ROBERT E. LEE'S LIGHTER SIDE

THE MARBLE MAN'S SENSE OF HUMOR

ROBERT E. LEE'S LIGHTER SIDE
THE MARBLE MAN'S SENSE OF HUMOR

COMPILED AND EDITED BY
THOMAS FOREHAND, JR.

PELICAN PUBLISHING COMPANY
Gretna 2006

Library of Congress Cataloging-in-Publication Data

Robert E. Lee's lighter side : the marble man's sense of humor /
edited by Thomas Forehand, Jr.
    p. cm.
Includes bibliographical references.
ISBN-13: 978-1-58980-355-8 (pbk. : alk. paper)
    1. Lee, Robert E. (Robert Edward), 1807-1870–Anecdotes. 2.
Lee, Robert E. (Robert Edward), 1807-1870–Quotations. 3. Lee,
Robert E. (Robert Edward), 1807-1870–Correspondence.   I.
Forehand, Thomas.
    E467.1.L4R59 2006
    973.7'42092–dc22

                                                    2005036390

Printed in the United States of America

Published by Pelican Publishing Company, Inc.
1000 Burmaster Street, Gretna, Louisiana 70053

For my kind and patient family:

Judy, Dana Carol, Thomas III, Rebecca, and Mama Ruth

Contents

Preface

"Marble" is often used to describe Robert E. Lee. That word does depict accurately one side of his personality. In public, he sat, stood, walked, and rode erect. In the presence of strangers, he armed himself with a quiet demeanor. Also, two wars and a military career, spanning five decades, honed his serious sense of duty toward God and man.

Yet like a cavalry screen, Lee's statuesque appearance obscured another side of his personality—his lighter side. Robert E. Lee consistently displayed a good sense of humor in what he said and wrote and in how he reacted to various situations. Those around Lee often had opportunities to laugh with him in the calm of peace as well as in the throes of war (even shortly before his surrender).

For those interested in learning more about Lee's lighter side, I have compiled more than one hundred examples of his good sense of humor. That humor budded in youth, bloomed before he became a soldier, and was still flowering on his last working day as president of Washington College.

Objects of General Lee's humor included: fellow soldiers, religious traditions (fasting, High Church/Low Church, etc.), newspaper editors, biographies, spiritualism, newborn babies (their number, their birthmarks, their gender), liquor, weddings, accidents, military rank, courtship, dating, honeymooning, pets, military chow, his personal appearance, his own celebrity, his wife, his children, doctors, medicine, politicians, studying, selfishness, pomp, handwriting, artists, weather, school absences, marriage, obeying orders, pipe smoking, kissing, spelling, and clothing.

Like most fathers, Lee romped and played games with his children; unlike most fathers, he enjoyed having them tickle his hands and feet.

During the war, he frequently shot bullets of humorous rebuke. After the war, he once acted so silly at home that a visitor cringed to see him in one of his unguarded moments. Lee was full of fun. He joked, teased, punned, told humorous stories, occasionally pulled pranks, and sometimes laughed himself to tears.

For those interested in more details about Lee and his family, I have noted, in the endnotes, some of the less frequently published points about the Lees. In the endnotes, I have also included such points as: Lee's connection to Napoleon's family; the Jim Crow law allegedly broken by one of Lee's daughters; the religious reason Mary Custis almost refused to marry Robert E. Lee; why Lee marched out of step in military parades after the war; one of the honors that the Federal government currently bestows on Lee; the Federal committee both Robert E. Lee and Abraham Lincoln were members of during the 1840s; and, Lee's near relative who was a general both in the Confederacy and later in the United States military.

Let's now pick the locks of Lee's heart by reading about his lighter side.

—Tom Forehand, Jr., Editor and Compiler

A Chronology of Events in Lee's Life

1807 Born January 19.

1818 Father dies.

1825 Enters the United States Military Academy at West Point.

1829 Graduates second in his class at West Point.

1831 Marries Mary Custis (great-granddaughter of Martha Washington).

Stationed at Fort Monroe in Virginia.

1834 Transferred to Washington, DC.

1835 Returns to Arlington after a summer expedition to Canada.

1837 Stationed in St. Louis.

1841 Stationed at Fort Hamilton (Brooklyn), New York.

1846 Leaves for the Mexican-American War.

1848 Returns to Arlington from Mexico and is stationed in Baltimore.

1852 Becomes the superintendent of the U.S. Military Academy at West Point.

1856 Arrives in Texas for a cavalry assignment.

1858 Writes to son Custis who is in California.

1859 Speeds, with Jeb Stuart, to Harper's Ferry to capture John Brown.

1861 Resigns from the United States Army and takes command of Virginia's military.

(The War Between the States begins.)

1862 Takes command of the Army of Northern Virginia and drives General George B. McClellan from the gates of Richmond.

Engages in the battle of Second Manassas in the summer.

1863 Engages in the battle of Gettysburg in the summer.

1864 Engages in the battle of the Wilderness in early May.

(General Ulysses S. Grant's siege of Petersburg begins in June.)

1865 Retreats to Appomattox and is forced to surrender to Grant in early April.

(The War Between the States soon ends.)

Accepts the presidency of Washington College in late August.

1870 Dies in Lexington, Virginia, on October 12.

1. The Best Confederate Generals

General Robert E. Lee, sporting a tongue-in-cheek attitude, informed Georgia's B. H. Hill about the Confederacy's best generals.

We made a great mistake, Mr. Hill, in the beginning of our struggle, and I fear in spite of all we can do, it will prove to be a fatal mistake. . . . Why, sir, in the beginning we appointed all our worst generals to command the armies, and all our best generals to . . . [do something else]. As you know, I have planned some campaigns and quite a number of battles. I have given the work all the care and thought I could, and sometimes, when my plans were completed, as far as I could see, they seemed to be perfect. But when I have fought them through, I have discovered defects and occasionally wondered [why] I did not see some of the defects in advance. When it was all over, I found by reading a newspaper that these best editor generals saw all the defects plainly from the start. Unfortunately, they did not communicate their knowledge to me until it was too late. . . . I have no ambition but to serve the Confederacy, and do all I can to win our independence. I am willing to serve in any capacity to which the authorities may assign me. I have done the best I could in the field, and have not succeeded as I could wish. I am willing to yield my place to these best generals, and I will do my best for the cause editing the newspaper.[1]

2. A New Way to Fast

Lee's religious views on fasting were more practical than traditional. "Discussing Lent, he said: 'The best way for most of us is to fast from our sins and to eat what is good for us.'"[2]

3. Fire Power

While Lee was president of Washington College, an explosive incident prompted his attention. After the new term opened, four students rented a campus room, which they used between class lectures. According to one of them, they used the room to stay warm; each would take his turn in purchasing a new supply of wood when it was needed. The wood was then cut into short lengths and stacked in a corner. The winter was cold with snow remaining "on the ground" for eleven straight weeks. It was Graham's time to purchase a new load of wood; soon the four noticed that the wood was disappearing at an alarming rate; so they naturally believed that someone was stealing it. With the school's wood stacked some two hundred feet from their room, and the janitor not being very industrious, Graham became even more suspicious and decided to set a trap for the wood thief. So, he chose a log, drilled a hole in it, and then filled the hole with gunpowder; finally he covered the hole with clay. Then Graham placed it on their woodpile and warned the others not to put that log in the stove. The next day, there was a loud explosion in Dr. J's room; his stove was blown apart, and the building was set on fire.

All of this activity created a commotion on campus. Before starting the chapel service, General Lee reminded the students that the faculty had set no rules for the student body and that each individual was assumed to be a gentleman. Lee also reminded the student body that their "honor" was to "control" what went on in campus life. The General allowed that he was willing to speak with anyone who knew details of the explosion. Graham was sure that it was his powdered log that had caused the blast. So late that morning, Graham and one of his partners journeyed to President Lee's office. When they went in to see General Lee, Graham told him about their plan to catch the thief. Then he bemoaned the fact that he had no idea there was any connection with the missing wood and Prof. J's room. Seldom had Graham's partner seen the General "laugh," yet Lee gently admonished, "Well, Mr. Graham, your plan to find out who was taking your wood was a good one, but your powder charge was too heavy." Lee urged Graham not to use as much powder the next time.[3]

4. True History

Lexington, Va. September 26, 1866 . . .

Dear Sir: I return to you my thanks for the compliment paid

me by your proposition to write a history of my life. It is a hazardous undertaking to publish the life of any one while living, and there are but few who would desire to read a *true* history of themselves. Independently of a few national events with which mine has been connected, it presents little to interest the general reader. . . .

Very respectfully, R. E. Lee[4]

5. Ask Caesar

A Washington College faculty member gave the following example of how Lee uniquely answered one letter from a medium.

[Lee] was always an agreeable companion. There was a good deal of bonhomie and pleasantry in his conversation. He was not exactly witty, nor was he very humorous, though he gave a light turn to table-talk and enjoyed exceedingly any pleasantry or fun, even. He often made a quaint or slightly caustic remark, but took care that it should not be too trenchant. On reading his letters one discovers this playful spirit in many of them, as, for instance, in his letter to the spiritualist who asked his opinion of Von Moltke and the French war. [Lee] wrote in reply a most courteous letter in which he said that "the question was one about which military critics would differ, that [my] own judgment about such matters was poor at best, and that inasmuch as [spiritualists] had the power to consult (through their mediums) Caesar, Alexander, Napoleon, Wellington, and all of the other great captains who had ever lived, [I] could not think of obtruding [my] opinion in such company." [5]

6. He's No Little Shaver

Since it was difficult to work during the winter, Robert E. Lee and his growing family stayed at Arlington, their family home in Virginia, across the Potomac River from Washington, DC. However, he returned to New York in early 1843 and tried to make speedy repairs because it seemed that Congress might cut funds for these efforts. His wife also went to New York but came back to Arlington that fall to deliver her sixth child. The little boy, born on October 27, 1843, was named after his father. Lee described him to a friend in St. Louis: "He has a fine long nose like his father, but no whiskers."[6]

7. Lee with His Children

Lee, most dignified in public, was more relaxed at home. His son Robert, Jr., recalled:

[I]t pleased and delighted [my father] to take off his slippers and place his feet in our laps. . . . Often, as little things, after romping all day, the enforced sitting would be too much for us, and our drowsiness would soon show itself in continued nods. Then, to arouse us, he had a way of stirring us up with his foot laughing heartily at and with us. He would often tell us the most delightful stories, and then there was no nodding. Sometimes, however, our interest in his wonderful tales became so engrossing that we would forget to do our duty when he would declare, "No tickling, no story!"[7]

8. Brandy, Anyone?

One of Lee's officers related:

With all his grandeur of character, his simplicity was almost childlike, and his relish of a joke hearty. To illustrate this, our old friend, Mrs. F., living about a mile from our headquarters, sent me one day a demijohn of buttermilk, which, knowing his fondness for it, I directed Bryan, our factotum, to take to the General's tent, with Mrs. F.'s compliments. At twelve o'clock, our usual lunch hour, the General had the demijohn brought out and put on the table with drinking-vessels, and then summoned the gentlemen of his staff. Seeing a *demijohn*, all imagined it to be a present of fine old Brandy or wine, of which rarity we were invited to partake, especially when the General ceremoniously said to the servant, "Bryan, help the gentlemen, Colonel——first . . ." (who he knew never drank buttermilk . . .). The eager expectation visible in each countenance was as much enjoyed by the General, as was the disappointment expressed when each tasted his cup; the wry faces made by some of the guests provoking a hearty laugh from the host.[8]

9. His Popular Hat

During the few times Lee traveled extensively after the war, he was often confronted by crowds of admirers and onlookers. As was the respectful custom, he would raise his hat above his head to salute the crowd. Returning from one such trip, the celebrity kidded with his daughter: "'[T]hey would make too much fuss over the old rebel.' A few days after he came home, one of his daughters remonstrated with him about the hat he was wearing. He replied: 'You don't like this hat? Why, I have seen a whole cityful [*sic*] come out to admire it.'"[9]

10. A Bridal Party Prank

The young-married Lee was stimulated by Washington, DC's social life. He recorded for his friends, the Talcotts, that he had returned to a state of youthfulness. What had done the trick? Not only had his brother Smith just married, but Lee had also attended a bridal party the previous evening. That is what he wanted to tell Mrs. Talcott about in particular. He wrote

> that my Spirits were so buoyant last night, when relieved from the eyes of my Dame, that my Sister [in-law] Nanie was trying to pass me off as her spouse, but I was not going to have my sport spoiled that way, [so I] undeceived [*sic*] the young ladies and told them I was her younger brother. Sweet, innocent things, they concluded I was single and I have not had such soft looks and tender pressure of the hand for many years.[10]

11. Top Hat: A Teapot Warmer

According to Mrs. Cornelius McDonald who frequently saw Lee in public, he always acted in a "courteous and elegant" way, and there seemed to be "a sort of unapproachable majesty about him."

However, one day Mrs. Susan P. Lee, his relative by marriage, saw another side of the man. General Lee received a lot of gifts. Two of these were "an afghan and teapot warmer shaped like an ancient helmet." With his daughter at the piano, Lee, the Southern icon, waltzed "into the room" sporting the teapot warmer on his head and bearing the afghan on his shoulders. Startled by the old warrior's performance, Susan quickly left the house and told others about the General's unexpected behavior.[11]

12. Jeb's Music

Lee constantly tried to keep his troops' morale as high as possible, especially the morale of those closest to him. He enjoyed jesting at meals and even during his inspections. One day during the fall of 1862, Lee could hear Sweeny, Jeb Stuart's well-known banjoist, entertaining a group of troops near his tent. When Lee came out to express his gratitude for the merriment, he noticed a jug of liquor and inquired dryly: "Gentlemen . . . am I to thank General Stuart or the jug for this fine music?"[12]

13. "Come In, Captain"

Lee did not allow the formation of an honor battalion because he was certain that the new unit would not be able to hold every man who was worthy of such distinction. Also, to each lowly private who wanted to speak with him, he was willing to grant an audience. On one particular day, he beckoned a private into his tent by calling him "Captain." Lee urged him to take a seat, but the private answered that he was not a captain. Then Lee repeated: "Come in sir . . . come in and take a seat. You ought to be a captain." Many years later, that private noted the sound confidence that Lee's soldiers had in him—such confidence that they would follow him anywhere.[13]

14. Prayers

A preacher at the college chapel services habitually prayed so long that his prayers extended into the time allotted for first-period lectures. So in an ironic yet practical way, Lee asked one of his professors: "Would it be wrong for me to suggest that he confine his morning prayers to us poor sinners at the college?" Lee felt that the preacher could pray for all of the various people around the world "some other time?"[14]

15. A Honeymoon or a Wake?

Robert E. Lee and his wife were unable to attend the wedding of one of Lee's closest friends. So they wrote congratulatory responses. Lee, with a light-and-easy attitude, wrote that he and his wife had wanted to attend the wedding, but their invitation arrived too late.[15] Then Lee seasoned his letter with a jolly statement to the new husband by branding him "Gilderoy," a thief, since he had apparently stolen Lee's old-time friend, the new bride Eliza Mackay.[16] Lee then compared marriage ceremonies with funerals and asked about the couple's honeymoon. Lee's wife then attached a more sober note of congratulations to the end of her husband's joyous letter.[17]

16. Not Kissable

During the war the Lees had no permanent home. So the Caskie family invited Lee's wife and daughters to live with them. Mr. Caskie, who was wealthy as a result of his activities in the tobacco industry, offered to aid Lee with any personal business. The Caskies had only one child, a daughter named Norvell, who was magnetic, with an uplifting spirit and a sharp mind, both of which soon attracted Lee's attention. This new friendship helped him regain his normal sense of humor suppressed by the recent death of his daughter. After he arrived at Culpeper, he started writing to Norvell. To his wife he soon wrote again with his normal lighthearted tendencies. In one such letter, he instructed Mary: "Tell Miss [Norvell] that I have scanned Major T. & T.'s faces with anxiety but they will not answer for my purpose. I could find nothing kissable in them." Lee jokingly admitted that he may not have looked at the men in the proper manner; however, he did send further instructions for Norvell not to recommend them again because when he compared her with them, it caused a revolution in nature! Lee, as a younger-married man, had once pretended to be a bachelor in order to receive attention from some belles at a party.

Though he had departed from such antics, he still liked the attention of pretty women, especially at social occasions. At such times, they would cluster around him, grab his hand gently, and listen joyously at his stories. He was most happy on such occasions and liked having the fatherly right to kiss these young ladies, many of whom he knew as toddlers. Once, when he was riding down Franklin Street in Richmond, he saw his daughter Mary besieged by an amorous lad. Lee noticed immediately that she was not interested in the boy's attention. So he stopped his horse, got off, walked up to Mary, and taunted the young man by giving her a kiss and then asking him if he would like to do what Lee had just done.[18]

17. Can't Spare It!

A rumor reached Richmond that Major Heros von Borcke had become a fatality during the battle of Chancellorsville. Actually, he was alive and still fighting for the Confederacy. When Virginia's governor asked Lee to send von Borcke's body to Richmond, Lee replied: "Can't spare it! It's in pursuit of [Union cavalry general George] Stoneman."[19]

18. A "Lie"

The day after the battle of Second Manassas (Bull Run), Lee was with his staff when they chanced upon a sergeant who had scavenged a pair of shoes from a dead Union soldier. Lee confronted the sergeant by asking him why he was separated from his unit. The soldier, who did not recognize General Lee, barked out that it was a personal matter. Then Lee accused the man of straggling and said that he deserved to be heartily punished. The sergeant retorted that he was not straggling and had left his unit only shortly before to find some shoes; he also explained that he had fought in the previous day's battle where he noticed that Lee, and other cavalrymen, had not been ready to charge the enemy once they had been put to flight. He turned the tables on Lee and accused him of laying back among the trees on the day of the battle instead of fighting. He also browbeat the General by accusing him of coming out, on the day after the battle, only because the danger had finally passed. Lee was speechless but surely laughing gently as he left the scene. One of the nearby officers then asked the sergeant if he knew who the man was that he had been speaking to. The sergeant said that he had been speaking to some cowardly Virginian. Then the officer pointed out that the sergeant had not been speaking to a coward but instead to General Robert E. Lee. The startled sergeant sputtered: "General Lee, did you say? . . . Scissors to grind, I'm a goner!" Then he took off in a hurry.[20]

19. Contagion

One afternoon two little girls, the daughters of two of his [college] professors, were riding on a gentle old horse up and down one of the back streets of [Lexington] . . . fearing to go far from home. The General, starting out on his afternoon ride, came up with them, knowing them well, said gaily:

"Come with me, little girls, and I will show you a beautiful ride." Only too delighted, they consented to go. He took them out beyond the fairgrounds, from which point there is one of the grandest stretches of mountain scenery in the world. One of the little maidens had her face tied up, as she was just recovering from the mumps. He pretended that he was much alarmed lest his horse should catch them from her, and kept saying: "I hope you won't give Traveller the mumps."[21]

20. Nauseous Water

At the springs where Lee was vacationing, two gentlemen from England would always walk with him around the place. Though he was fond of the English, Lee did not like this constant display of "hero worship" that proved "embarrassing." Later, the prankster Lee explained to a friend how he taught these two interlopers a lesson—how he got even with them. When the two met with him for his stroll, he would escort them "to the springs" and encourage them to imbibe the water, but not just any water. He said: "They are too polite to refuse when I hand them the glasses, and I fill them up with the nauseous water, and thus have my revenge."[22]

21. Lee Was Hit, but Not Hurt

During the winter of 1862-63, the esprit de corps of Lee's army should have been at its lowest ebb due to a lack of supplies and an abundance of freezing weather. Still, Lee was confident that his army's morale was as high as it had ever been. Near the end of January, with a blanket of deep snow spread across the ground, his troops fought a battle among themselves using frozen snowballs as ammunition! Thousands on each side waged this cold war. Even high-ranking officers spurred their men on in this spontaneous affair; these officers were not exempt from becoming casualties as they rode along lines of battle stretching for miles. The snowballs were often heaved so hard that their impact could spill blood or even break a limb. One particular day, General Evander McIvor Law's brigade traveled three miles to fight General Micah Jenkins's men who had depleted their stockpile of ammunition. Though the next day, Jenkins's men retaliated. Up early, bent on settling the score, and carrying a fresh supply of snowballs, they sneaked an attack on Law's men preparing to eat. With the sound of "who-who-ey! who-who-ey," Law's troops were routed and had to forfeit their early morning meal. A portion of that battle was pitched near Lee's headquarters. When the General stepped out of his tent to reconnoiter, even he became a casualty by sustaining several direct hits.[23]

22. Honest Meat?

At the siege of Petersburg, Colonel John S. Mosby, well-known for capturing enemy supplies, laid over at Edge Hill during February. He noticed that Lee was "not only kind but affectionate." Lee persuaded the colonel to join him for dinner, but warned the colonel that the meal might be sparse. When mutton was placed before the men, Lee, with his good sense of humor overflowing, suggested that the meat had been stolen![24]

During the winter of 1862-63, Lee seldom lost a chance to use humor for the purpose of raising his men's morale. When General John B. Hood and Colonel Robert H. Chilton were talking about methods of keeping their troops from pilfering pigs and wrecking fence rails, General Hood felt compelled to dismiss such accusations against his own men. Listening silently, Lee remarked: "Ah, General Hood, when you Texans come about, the chickens have to roost mighty high."[25]

23. Lee's Math: X + Y = Headache

General Porter Alexander recalled one of Lee's jollier moments. Alexander remembered visiting one evening with Colonel Talcott when they both started a discussion about mathematics; soon the two returned to their tent to solve a particular math problem. In the tent was Colonel Marshall, also a mathematician. Before long a "demijohn" was brought out and drinks offered. Yet, only Colonel Marshall imbibed at that time. Marshall humorously and adroitly acted like a clown and poured the whiskey over one of his shoulders into his glass. Not only did he try to give the impression of being a tough guy, but the other two feared that he was going to drink all the whiskey. At that moment, General Lee looked into the tent and observed Marshall's antics. The next day when Marshall lamented the pains in his head, General Lee gave this mathematical analysis: "Too much application to mathematical problems at night, with the unknown quantities x & y represented by a demijohn & tumbler, was very apt to have for a result a head ache [*sic*] next morning."[26]

24. Not Shot, Yet

A man, who waited a long time to see General Lee, identified himself as a soldier. General Lee must have brandished a hidden grin when he asked him some questions. First, Lee asked him if he was a soldier in the Northern army or in the Southern army. The man replied that he was a member of Lee's army. Then the General asked him if he had ever been shot. The man replied that he had not. Finally Lee asked: "How is that? Nearly all of our men get shot." The man explained that he had not been shot yet because he always stayed back where the generals stayed! Lee liked to tell his staff this story and did so more than once.[27]

25. Never Marry a Preacher

Lee, with genial joviality, gave some advice when he wrote home during the Mexican-American War. He not only poked fun at those in Alexandria, Virginia, who were getting married, he also singled out one lass in particular: "Tell Miss—— she had better dismiss that young [preacher] and marry a soldier. There is some chance of the latter being shot, but it requires a particular dispensation of Providence to rid her of the former."[28]

26. Ug-Lee

In June 1862, Lee wrote to his daughter-in-law and described himself by using the humorous overstatement or hyperbole "ugly."

And now I must answer your inquiries about myself. My habiliments are not as comfortable as yours, nor so suited to this hot weather, but they are the best I have. My coat is of gray, of the regulation style and pattern, and my pants of dark blue, as is also prescribed, partly hid by my long boots. I have the same handsome hat which surmounts my gray head (the latter is not prescribed in the regulations) and shields my ugly face, which is masked by a white beard as stiff and wiry as the teeth of a card. In fact, an uglier person you have never seen, and so unattractive is it to our enemies that they shoot at it whenever visible to them, but though age with its snow has whitened my head, and its frosts have stiffened my limbs, my heart, you well know, is not frozen to you, and summer returns when I see you.[29]

27. A Good Kind of Coward

According to Robert, Jr., he and his father were visiting at the home of a Dr. Tabb after the war.

Mr. Graves, Dr. Tabb's overseer, who had the honour of being the coachman, fully appreciated it, and was delighted when my father praised his management. He had been a soldier under the General, and had stoutly carried his musket to Appomatox [*sic*], where he surrendered it. When told of this by Dr. Tabb, my father took occasion to compliment him on his steadfast endurance and courage, but Graves simply and sincerely replied, "Yes, General, I stuck to the army, but if you had in your entire command a greater coward than I was, you ought to have had him shot." My father, who was greatly amused at his candour, spoke of it when he got back from his drive, saying, "that sort of coward makes a good soldier."[30]

28. Horsing Around

During the early 1830s, Lee was riding his horse on Pennsylvania Avenue in Washington, DC. While nearing a fellow officer on foot, Lee joyfully roared: "Come, get up with me." After his friend boarded the startled animal, both of them continued along the avenue. More startled than the poor horse was the near-by Secretary of the Navy! He not only witnessed the event, but also told his brother, at the War Department, about this unexpected antic—an antic that he felt lacked dignity![31]

29. Tough Biscuits

During the winter of 1862-63, Lee and his men met one of their staunchest enemies—hunger. Though his soldiers were often starving, Lee was diligent to remain peppy and upbeat for their benefit. He would boost their temperaments by turning a complaint about food into a jest. When one aide spoke of the hardness of a biscuit, Lee responded: "You ought not to mind that. They will stick by you the longer."[32]

30. New York City Danger

In the early 1840s, Lee was stationed at Fort Hamilton in Brooklyn, New York. Before Mrs. Lee joined him, he surely giggled when he wrote to her that she could get anything she wanted in the city; however, he warned there were so many pretty things in the stores that it was "dangerous" to go into any of them.[33] At times, Lee would pick at his wife for being careless with her time and her money. He wrote to his son that she thought "herself to be a great financier." However, he also warned: "Consult her about the expenditure of money, but do not let her take it shopping, or you will have to furnish her with an equal amount to complete her purchases."[34]

31. A Fine "Howdy Do"

At Cold Harbor, Lee was highly visible when he rode among his troops. Though his mount Traveller was well groomed, Lee's clothing was "as simple as" that of his soldiers. He was unarmed and seldom accompanied by more than one other soldier. Once when "a feebleminded soldier" addressed the General with "Howdy do, dad," Lee responded, "Howdy do, my man."[35]

32. Death at the Lighthouse

During 1835, a summer expedition took Lee to Canada's Pelee Island. He and a fellow army engineer, Washington Hood, were to locate accurately Ohio's northern boundary. Lee wrote of their deadly encounter while trying to enter a lighthouse at the island's southern tip. His humor was ripe as he recorded their adventure. The lighthouse door was locked, so Lee and Hood entered through a window. It was there they encountered the "keeper" whom Lee described as "irascible & full of venom." Immediately a clash took place; Lee and Hood survived, but their opponent was killed. The two soldiers confiscated several glass lampshades to replace their broken ones. Since these articles belonged to the Canadian government, Lee said that he would later apologize to Canada's minister in Washington, DC. Concerning their dead opponent: Lee thought they had actually done Canada a service by killing him. So Lee wanted to advise the minister next time "to make choice of a better subject than a . . . Canadian *Snake*." One Lee scholar, upon reading this letter, believed that Lee and his comrade had actually killed a Canadian lighthouse keeper. Yet, Lee was simply writing a lighthearted commentary about confronting and killing a real reptile.[36]

33. A Bible, Use It!

Lexington, Virginia, September 5, 1866

A. J. Requier

81 Cedar St., New York

My Dear Sir: I am very much obliged to you for your kind letter of the 22nd ult [*sic*]. So many articles formerly belonging to me are scattered over the country that I fear I have not time to devote to their recovery. I know no one in Buffalo whom I could ask to reclaim the Bible in question. If the lady who has it will use it, as I hope she will, she will herself seek to restore it to the rightful owner. I will, therefore, leave the decision of the question to her and her conscience. . . .

With great respect,

Your obedient servant,

R. E. Lee[37]

34. Streams, Rivulets, and Brooks

On November 24, 1860, a few weeks after Lincoln had been elected president, a melancholy Lee wrote to his son Custis about the country's precarious condition. Yet, intermingled with these burdening thoughts was Lee's play on words about the Brooks family.

Mrs. Brooks, the wife of the Major, has adhered to her husband, and though they are encamped about three or four miles from town, she declines the protection of a house and remains in camp. She rode up Saturday and I brought her into the office to warm herself while the Major was adjusting his papers. She seems to be a very nice lady. Was [*sic*] a Miss Drake of Indiana, and I am told is quite an heiress. She would not dine with me, nor accept a room at Mrs. Phillips, but returned with . . . Major [Phillips] to camp. I did not hear or see anything of any little streams or rivulets and hesitated to ask.[38]

35. You Protest Too Much!

Lee's seriousness was often mixed with a little levity when he had to counsel some of his wayward college students. One particular student had too many unexcused absences from his classes. The day of reckoning finally came when he was ordered to General Lee's office. The student was horrified, anticipating his audience with the patriarch of the campus. However, General Lee was very nice to the young man and asked gentle questions. Soon the student blurted out several reasons why he had missed class. First he said that he had been ill; but quickly realizing that he looked very healthy, he tried another excuse. The second excuse was that he had left his shoes at the repair shop. After all his stammering and meandering, President Lee interjected: "Stop Sir! One good reason is enough." Upon hearing that statement, the student thought he saw a "twinkle" in Lee's eyes.[39]

36. High Church/Low Church Controversy

Lee was stationed with his family in New York.

A fellow soldier, Lieutenant Henry Hunt, recalled how much Lee's small clan had become part of their "little society." Lee, he allowed, had been a "vestryman" of the small church parish at Fort Hamilton. Lieutenant Hunt noted a particular church dispute; it was between those who favored the more traditional "Low-Church" view and those who favored the new "High-Church" view. Though Lee was a Low Churcher, he did not want to become part of the dispute (even though both sides wanted to gain his support). Hunt reported that such attempts to win Lee over always failed. Lee tried to stir clear of a situation where he would have to give an opinion that favored either side. In the midst of the controversy, Lee's humor took the day. One evening he visited some officers who were members of the parish; when he arrived, he found that they had been joined by some civilians. The subject for discussion was the hot issue of Low Church versus High Church. Lee was entertained by their attempts to elicit his opinion on the subject; still, he preferred to stay out of a dispute that was upsetting church members who needed to work together. However, he agreed to make one statement about the matter. No doubt to the surprise and amazement of all, in that statement he poked fun at the whole debate! Lee's lightheartedness, in the midst of a serious situation, made such an impression that Hunt recalled it later during the Mexican-American War.[40]

37. Ill

Not long after the Civil War, the Lees lived temporarily in the country—far from the hustle and bustle of Richmond. The small, rustic house loaned to them was called Derwent. There, Robert, Jr., took care of his mother and sisters until they moved to Lexington. Robert, Jr., not used to crop labor in the fields, began to suffer repeatedly from symptoms of malaria. He developed chills that lasted for long periods. His father did not hesitate to tease young Robert, Jr., about the new illness and did so by giving him a new nickname. He took Robert, Jr.'s, former nickname of "Robertus" (or "Bertus") and changed it to the more up-to-date nickname of "Robertus Sickus."[41]

Lee's second daughter, Annie, was born in 1839. His wife was worried about the newborn because the baby girl bore a red birthmark on her face. Though Mrs. Lee hoped the mark would disappear, it gave every indication of remaining. Outwardly, Lee poked fun at his wife by claiming that the mark was caused by "some *whim wham* of that *Mama*." By saying this, he was referring to the superstition that "nervous" or scared women delivered "abnormal" children. He even gave his daughter a pet name: "Little Raspberry." Outwardly, he joked about the situation, but inwardly, he was worried about the future appearance of the child.[42]

38. The Tennessee Line

The day before Lee surrendered his Army of Northern Virginia to General Grant, he had been trying to outdistance Grant's closely trailing force. After a long day of retreat, all seemed to be peaceful that night in Lee's camp when a messenger from General John Gordon appeared. Gordon, expecting that Lee's army would all break through Grant's blocking movement the next day, had sent the messenger to inquire where they were to camp for the night. Breaking the tension of impending disaster, Lee's mother wit rose to the occasion: "Tell General Gordon I should be glad for him to halt just beyond the Tennessee line." The Tennessee line was about 175 miles from their position.[43]

39. Pickin' On a Slow Poke

When the Lees lived in Baltimore in the early 1850s, the children grew used to seeing their parents leave for the evening to attend social functions. Robert, Jr., recalled that his father was "always in full uniform, always ready and waiting for my mother, who was generally late. He would chide her gently, in a playful way and with a bright smile."[44]

40. An Incurable Disease

From the battle of Fredericksburg until his death, Lee may have suffered from intermittent heart problems. Toward the end of his life, he struggled when modeling for E. V. Valentine. At times, Valentine would see Lee touch his chest as if he felt pain from the heart. Yet, he murmured no complaint. The closest Lee came to complaining was when he requested that his son Custis model in his place (since the son looked very much like his father). When the sculptor came to bid his last farewell to Lee, he found the General chattering away in the parlor. There, Lee stoically and ironically diagnosed the cause of all his health problems: "I feel that I have an incurable disease coming on—old age."[45]

41. Cruel Stonewall

Thomas Jonathan "Stonewall" Jackson was often the target of a joke by Robert E. Lee, Jeb Stuart, or James Longstreet. While near Hayfield, Virginia, Stonewall stopped to call on one of his relatives, Mrs. W. P. Taylor, who had two young women with her. When Stonewall and others arrived, General Lee told the group that he had brought his best generals for the women to admire, and had permitted his young officers to come to admire the women. While Jackson watched, Lee then told Mrs. Taylor that Stonewall was a man of utmost cruelty and inhumanity. Lee continued by saying that at the battle of Fredericksburg, he had scarcely restrained Stonewall "from putting bayonets on the guns of his men and driving all those people into the river." To which Mrs. Taylor retorted that it was her understanding that General Jackson was a Christian; and, she wished that if "those people" came to Hayfield, General Lee would do nothing to prevent Stonewall from pushing them back.[46]

42. Here a Lee, There a Lee

Lee wrote to his youngest son Robert, Jr., on January 17, 1864. At that time, his son was stationed with the cavalry near Charlottesville.

Tell Fitz [my nephew] I grieve over the hardship and sufferings of his men in their expedition. I would have preferred his waiting for more favorable weather. He accomplished much under the circumstances, but would have done more in better weather. I am afraid he was anxious to get back to the ball. This is a bad time for such trivial amusements. I would rather his officers should entertain themselves in fattening their horses, healing their men, and recruiting their regiments. There are too many Lees on the committee. I like them all to be present at battles, but can excuse them at balls. But the saying is "Children will be children."[47]

43. Wigwam on the Potomac

Robert E. Lee, Jr., described his father's lighthearted spirit while at home with the children.

He was always bright and gay with us little folk, romping, playing, and joking with us. With the older children, he was just as companionable, and I have seen him join with my elder brothers and their friends when they would try their powers at a high jump put up in our yard. The two younger children he petted a great deal, and our greatest treat was to get into his bed in the morning and lie close to him, listening while he talked to us in his bright and entertaining way.[48]

Near summer when the temperatures climbed, the Lee children were able to go outside more often. This was a relief to Lee who believed that such outdoor play lessened "the confusion in the Wigwam." Also, at times he would frolic so much with his little children that he felt like "a horse, dog, ladder, and target for cannon."[49]

44. Powwow

On the last working day of Lee's life, shortly before he died, his sense of humor was fully alive. That morning, September 28, 1870, he conversed with students, penned a letter, and autographed a photo. Early in the afternoon, he plodded up the hill to his new house for a meal, took a siesta, and then walked to church for a vestry meeting. Before he left home, he heard his daughter Mildred, nicknamed "Life," playing Felix Mendelssohn's "Songs without Words." Her next piano tune was the "Funeral March." It was the second song that brought a response from the old General: "Life, that is a doleful piece you are playing." He was not keen on going to church that night because he did not want to have to "listen to all that powpow" or business to be discussed. He kissed his daughter, as he always did before leaving, then walked to church in the rain. That night when he returned home, he never left it again alive.[50]

45. Housekeeping

When Lee was on duty at Fort Monroe in the 1830s, his wife sewed, cared for their baby, superintended a few servants and the cooking and cleaning. Yet at times, Robert poked fun at her for not being industrious enough. He even told a friend that his wife was addicted both to forgetting her housework and being lazy. However, he concluded: "[S]he does her best, or in her mother's words, 'The Spirit is willing but the flesh is weak.'"[51]

According to author John Perry, there may have been some truth in Lee's analysis. Yet, this was Mary's first time to live away from her folks, as well as her first time to keep house without a large number of servants helping. Perry compares Mary's stay at Fort Monroe with "the nineteenth-century version of government housing."[52]

46. The Minister's Grace

When Lee was president of Washington College, he liked a good pun. Since he understood why young men often attended church, he was not surprised to hear a lament by General W. N. Pendleton, the local Episcopal rector. The minister was aggravated because some of his male members, students at the college, were attending Presbyterian services instead. Dr. Pratt, the Presbyterian minister, was not only an eloquent speaker, but he also had an attractive daughter named Grace. So when the rector explained that his young men were apparently attracted by Dr. Pratt's eloquent sermons, Lee countered: "I rather think . . . that the attraction is not so much Doctor Pratt's eloquence as it is Doctor Pratt's Grace."[53]

47. Healthy Studying

When a visitor asked about a particular student at the college, President Lee quipped:

> He is a very quiet, orderly young man, but seems very careful *not to injure the health of his father's son.* He got last month only forty on his Greek, thirty-five on his Mathematics, forty-seven on his Latin, and fifty on his English, which is a very low stand, as one hundred is our maximum. Now, I do not want our young men to really injure their health [by studying]; but I wish them to come as near it as possible.[54]

During exams, Lee surely felt like chuckling when he observed one student's attempt to remember the correct answers. When the young man began to stare quietly and pensively at the professor, Lee softly explained to a visitor: "He's trying to absorb it from Mr. Humphreys," a brilliant Washington College student.[55]

48. Wedding or Funeral?

Mary Custis and Robert E. Lee were married on a rainy day, the last day of June 1831. Six bridesmaids and six groomsmen accompanied the pair into one of the large downstairs rooms at the Arlington mansion. Lee recalled that Mary's hand trembled and that the minister spoke "as if he had been reading my Death [*sic*] warrant."[56]

49. Where's the Beef?

Lee was "particularly sensitive to greediness" and was "not diplomatic" about rebuking it. On one occasion, a corps commander and his aide ate with General Lee. A plate of greens with a single piece of beef was placed before them. The commander was satisfied with some of the vegetables, yet his greedy aide asked for beef. When Lee offered him beef, the aide took it all. On a later occasion, Lee ate a meal with the same two; this time the corps commander provided the food that included roast beef. When Lee was asked what he wanted from the table, he smiled at the selfish aide and taunted: "I will thank you for a piece of beef, if Captain S——— does not want all of it."[57]

50. The Unstoppable Pickett

When Grant's army began to press Petersburg in June 1864, Lee had sent orders to prevent an unnecessary attack involving General George E. Pickett's men; yet, Lee's orders arrived too late. Afterward, when Lee learned that Pickett's attack had been successful, he wrote General Richard Anderson a note of gratitude. According to renowned Lee biographer Douglas Southall Freeman, this note was unique; among Lee's official dispatches of this type, it was "almost" the only one where Lee displayed humor (along with his unbounded confidence in the troops). In that note Lee congratulated General Anderson for the way his men had acted and affirmed his confidence that they could take any position they faced. Then Lee, with tongue in cheek, apologized: "We tried very hard to stop Pickett's men from capturing the breastworks of the enemy, but couldn't do it. I hope his loss has been small."[58]

51. Cannibal Lee

While Lee was on an unexpectedly long expedition in 1835, his daughter Mary was born. For many months, his wife suffered from a post-delivery illness. As can be seen in his letters, after returning home Lee's spirits seesawed. One epistle would exhibit happiness, the next depression. Yet, the long winter of his wife's illness soon led into a springtime of recovery—a recovery not only of his wife's health but also of his own sagging spirits. Evidence of his recovered humor is found in a gaily written letter that mentioned the mansion hill's greenery and the garden flowers' perfumery. Yet, he was especially thinking of his little girl. "Oh, she is a rare one, and if only sweet sixteen, I would wish myself a cannibal that I might eat her up." He then claimed that he gave "all the young ladies a holyday [*sic*], and [would] hurry home to her every day."[59]

52. Lee's Complaint

In 1849, Mary Custis Lee and six of the Lee children moved into a new Baltimore rental house. Downstairs the multistory row house on Madison Avenue had a kitchen, a dining room, and two parlors. Upstairs there were several bedrooms, another room that could pass for a library, and a servants' quarters. Because windows only faced the front and back of the house, indoor sunlight was a premium. Even though it was a large house compared with most in the city, Lee complained that it was "hardly big enough to swing a cat in."[60]

53. Rapping, Rapping, Gently Rapping

A few months before the battle of Gettysburg, an ill Lee joshed when he wrote to his wife that an illness had forced him to lodge in a private residence. There he recuperated in a cozy room while a servant named Perry waited on him. His aches, which came in spasms, were in the back, chest, and arms. Even though most of his pain had subsided by the time he wrote, he still had a small fever and was having to use copious amounts of quinine. He pointed out that his doctors were "very attentive & kind & have examined my lungs, my heart, circulation, &c. . . . They have been rapping me all over like an old steam boiler before condemning it."[61]

54. Just Some Civilians

Robert E. Lee, Jr., recalled:

A young friend who was a cadet at the Virginia Military Institute [adjacent to the Washington College campus where we lived] called on my sisters one evening, and remarked. . . . "Do you know this is the first civilian's house I have entered in Lexington." My father was in the room in his gray Confederate coat shorn of the buttons, also my two brothers, Custis and Fitzhugh, both of whom had been generals in the Confederate Army; so there was quite a laugh over the term *civilian*.[62]

55. Politicians

In St. Louis, Lee penned a note of humorous sarcasm about politicians. The "Vani-tes" he noted, had won the state's election. (Even though the Whigs had won the local one.) He also noted that "the great *expunger*," Thomas Hart Benton, would be back in Congress denouncing "banks, bribery & corruption." Yet, Lee more particularly roasted the vain promises of wealth that were made by politicians. "While on the river I cannot help being on the lookout for that stream of gold that was to ascend the Mississippi River, tied up in silk-net purses!" Lee claimed that this tide of gold might be a beautiful sight, but he had not yet seen it as far north as St. Louis.[63]

56. Bob and the Nabob

When Lee was working on the Mississippi River in the late 1830s, he poked fun at one Des Moines man whom he labeled "the nabob." Lee reported that he and another soldier walked a mile to Des Moines; there they met the whole population, which seemed to be one man, named Allen. Lee described him as "a hard featured man of about fifty . . . a large talker, [who] has the title of *Doctor*, whether of Law, Medicine or Science, I have never learned but I infer all three."[64]

57. R. E. Lee, MD

Lee had reservations about doctors and their medicines. His prescription for an ill friend: "Avoid all medicine as much as possible, adhere strictly to the diet & course of life that you find agrees with you & give yourself a *fair chance*. Esculapius himself could not have given you a more learned prescription or Polonius better advice to his son."[65]

58. Fighting Dirty

One story, that Lee told with "relish," occurred during the Mexican-American War.[66]

At the siege of Vera Cruz, Captain [Robert E. Lee was] ordered to throw up such works as were necessary to protect a battery which was to be manned by the sailors of a certain man-of-war, and to use these gallant tars in constructing the work. The time being short, [Lee,] the young engineer[,] pushed on the work very rapidly, and the sons of Neptune began to complain loudly, "They did not enlist to dig dirt, and they did not like to be put under a 'land-lubber' anyhow." At last, the captain of the frigate, a thorough specimen of a United States naval officer in the palmy days of the service, came to Captain Lee and remonstrated, and then protested against the "outrage" of putting his men to digging dirt. "The boys don't want any dirt to hide behind," said the brave old tar, with deep earnestness and not a few expletives; "they only want to *get at the enemy*; and after you have finished your banks we will not stay behind them, we will get up on top, where we can have a fair fight." Captain Lee quietly showed his orders, assured the old salt that he meant to carry them out, and pushed on [with] the work, amid curses both loud and deep. Just about the time the work was completed, the Mexicans opened upon that point a heavy fire, and these gallant sons of the sea were glad enough to take refuge behind their despised "bank of dirt. . . ." Not long afterward the gallant captain, who by-the-way [*sic*], was something of a character, met Captain

Lee, and, feeling that some apology was due him, said: "Well! I reckon you were right. I suppose the dirt *did* save some of my boys from being killed or wounded. But I knew that we would have no use for dirt-banks on shipboard, that there what we want is clear decks and an open sea. And the fact is, captain, I don't like this land-fighting anyway—*it ain't clean!*"[67]

59. Better Ask the Enemy to Wait

Late in 1861, Lee was charged with the task of strengthening Confederate southern coastal defenses, so he left Savannah for Amelia Island; there he saw that protection for the island was "poor indeed." Realizing that everyone did not like the backbreaking work involved in such military construction, he was still hopeful that something could be done since he had been able to hire enough people for at least a month. Then he expressed this desire: "I hope the enemy will be polite enough to wait for us. It is difficult to get our people to realize their position."[68]

60. How Real Soldiers Don't Eat

During the 1862 holiday season at Corbin Hall, a nearby plantation, Lee ate Christmas dinner with Generals Jackson, Pendleton, and Stuart. The meal was served in the plantation office. Lee was amused at the decorations because they were not fitting according to Stonewall Jackson's tastes. Similar to most farmers in the area, the Virginian Corbins were sports-minded; so they were prone to display, on the office walls, their traps, fishing gear, and deer antlers. These walls also held decorations including engraved images of both well-known race horses and well-bred canines. Not only was Stonewall adorned with new clothing, but his waiter entered sporting a white apron. After being seated, they saw a feast of various meats brought in by Mrs. Corbin. Lee laughingly mentioned Jackson's "style" and remarked that if Jackson really wanted to learn how honest-to-goodness soldiers toughened it out, he should come to eat with General Lee. These jests mounted when General Stuart found an impression of a fighting bird in his butter and thus connected it to Stonewall's "moral degeneracy."[69]

61. The House of Stuart

One day Lee was honored by a review of his cavalry, which he said looked "splendid." Both men and horses had recovered since "last Fall." Even Jeb Stuart appeared to be "in all his glory." When some young ladies placed a wreath of greenery on the neck of Stuart's mount, Lee warned the flamboyant cavalryman to be careful: "That is the way General [John] Pope's horse was adorned when he went to battle at Manassas!" Lee then signaled Traveller, and left with his generals at a fast pace in front of a long line of cavalry. Without hesitation, when he reached the end of the line three miles away, he turned with his escort and hurried back.[70]

62. Lee: The Rebel

Shortly before the battle of Gettysburg, Lee's army was marching northward. A Northern lady stopped by Lee's headquarters because she had been drawn by both her need for food and the sadness in his face. On the spur of the moment, she asked the General for his autograph. Hesitating, he replied: "Do you want the autograph of a Rebel?" He capitulated and wrote his name on a piece of paper for her. Then speaking of the war's cruel nature, he told her: "My only desire is that they will let me go home and eat my own bread in peace."[71]

63. Love and War

About the time General Grant reached Petersburg, Lee enclosed some advice in one of his letters. He wrote: "I am glad to hear of Miss Carrie Mason again. I feared the Philistines [Union troops] had her." Lee stated that it was a strange coincidence that she and Colonel Jenifer always seemed to be in Richmond at the same time! Lee sent instructions for her to "put away her idols" and "devote herself" to the Confederacy. "If she wants to do a good thing, tell her to come & see me."[72]

64. Protect the Mrs.!

One day, General Lee took aim and hit the bull's-eye with one of his keen-witted rebukes at Petersburg.

General Lee, who never suffered a day to pass without visiting some part of his lines, rode by the quarters of one of his major-generals, and requested him to ride with him. As they were going he asked General—— if a certain work which he had ordered to be pushed was completed. He replied with some hesitation that it was, and General Lee then proposed that they should go and see it. Arriving at the spot it was found that little or no progress had been made since they were there a week before, and General—— was profuse in his apologies, saying that he had not seen the work since they were there together, but that he had ordered it to be completed at once, and that Major—— had informed him that it had been already finished. General Lee said nothing then, except to remark, quietly, "We must give our personal attention to the lines." But, riding on a little farther, he began to compliment General—— on the splendid charger he rode. "Yes, sir," said General——, "he is a splendid animal, and I prize him the more highly because he belongs to my wife, and is her favorite riding-horse." "A magnificent horse," rejoined General Lee "but I should not think him safe for Mrs.—— to ride. He is entirely too spirited for a lady, and I would urge you by all means to take some of the mettle out of him before you suffer Mrs.—— to ride him again. And, by-the-way [sic], general, I would suggest to you that these rough paths along these *trenches would be very admirable ground over which to tame him.*" The face of the gallant soldier turned crimson; he felt most keenly the rebuke, and never afterward reported the condition of his lines upon information received from Major—— or any one else. His spirited charger felt the effect of this hint from headquarters.[73]

65. Cousin Markie

Lee enjoyed repeating his daughter's play on words about cousin Martha Custis "Markie" Williams. Markie had sent him a gift of several new handkerchiefs that she had monogrammed with his initials. His letter stated that he thought about rebuking her for the new handkerchiefs. Why? Because it would be painful to part with his four old ones that had been like old friends going through the thick and thin of war with him. Yet, he praised Martha's embroidery: "So splendidly have you succeeded, that Mildred proposes your appellation be changed from Mark*ie* to Mark*er*. You see how bright is the wit of the establishment."[74]

66. Just a Little Thing

Lee's nephew George was aware that his uncle was often primed for a jest or a good play on words. When the "petite" Miss Long came to stay with the Lees, her charms captured the heart of a certain young fellow. He was so ensnared that he came to see Miss Long more than once each day. Lee's nephew must have appreciated his uncle's evaluation of this love-smitten young man. Uncle Robert pronounced: "Yes, he is different from most men. . . . He wants but little here below, but he wants that little Long!"[75]

67. Right Writin'

Lee jocularly reported to his daughter Mildred about the family's vain attempt to read her handwriting.

We held a family council over [your letter]. It was passed from eager hand to hand and attracted wondering eyes and mysterious looks. It produced few words but a great deal of thinking, and the conclusion arrived at, I believe unanimously, was that there was a great fund of amusement and information in it if it could be extracted. I have therefore determined to put it carefully away till your return, seize a leisure day, and get you to interpret it. Your mother's commentary, in a suppressed soliloquy, was that you had succeeded in writing a wretched hand. Agnes thought that it would keep this cold weather—her thoughts running on jellies and oysters in the storeroom; but I, indignant at such aspersions upon your accomplishments, retained your epistle and read in an elevated tone an interesting narrative of travels in sundry countries, describing gorgeous scenery, hairbreadth escapes, and a series of remarkable events by flood and field, not a word of which they declared was in your letter. Your return, I hope, will prove the correctness of my version of your annals.[76]

68. An Ill Artist

After the war, artist Edward Valentine visited Lexington to sculpt a bust of President Lee. Lee was cordial and escorted the sculptor into town to help him find a place to lodge. Along the way, Lee joked with a few people. When Valentine witnessed Lee's easygoing style, he recalled what others had told him about the General's simple and gentle nature. Since Lee seemed to be so carefree, Valentine became less anxious about having to be cooped up with such an icon. As the two grew to know each other better, their conversations turned to even more personal matters. Valentine once spoke of digestive problems caused by the limestone water. He had even been to Dr. Graham, who had recommended a particular medicine that brought him some relief. Lee sprightly analyzed the situation and said: "I think you work much better when you have the dysentery on you. I must tell your doctor to keep it up." Both Lee and Valentine soon felt free to joke with one another.[77]

69. Art for Art's Sake

During May 1870, Lee paid a visit to the "studio" of the young sculptor Edward Valentine. He measured Lee carefully in preparation for a bust. Valentine told the General that his art business was not doing so well after the war. To which the General, in half-jest and half-seriousness, replied: "[A]n artist ought not to have much money."[78]

44

70. A Duck Day

Lee was willing to be seen carrying a grocery basket full of food, but he would not be seen using an umbrella, even in a downpour. Those who lived in Lexington could seldom predict what the General might say or do. One student, who was walking through the rain, unexpectedly stopped in front of Lee. The General's shoulders were draped with a gray "cape," his face covered with a "silver" beard, and his head surmounted by a wide-brimmed "campaign hat"—all of which gave an air of "military dignity." The youth had paused as if he were standing at "attention." Then Lee asked him about several women whom he had signed pictures for, as a favor to this lad. The youth replied that everything had turned out all right; he then began to make another comment when General Lee abruptly said, "This is a good day for ducks. Good-by." Then he left.[79]

71. "Bobby Lee"

One day Lee called on the wife of General A. P. Hill. Their little girl met him "at the door and exclaimed with that familiarity which the kind-hearted old hero had taught her: 'O General Lee, here is 'Bobby Lee' (holding up a puppy); 'do kiss him.' The general pretended to do so, and the little creature was delighted."[80]

72. An Opinion

"One of his generals once tried, in a confidential interview, to get General Lee to express himself in reference to a certain . . . officer about whom he himself spoke very freely. But the old chief [Lee] merely replied, with a quiet smile: 'Well, sir, if that is your opinion of General——, I can only say that you differ very widely from the general himself.'"[81]

73. Permission Denied

[Lee] had a quiet humor in administering his rebukes which made them very keenly felt. . . . After the battle of Malvern

Hill had ceased, and McClellan had left . . . for Harrison's Landing, one of the Confederate commanders, who had not been fortunate in his management of the attack, and was not aware that McClellan had retreated, galloped up to General Lee and exclaimed with considerable vehemence: "If you will permit me, sir, I will charge that hill with my whole force and carry it at the point of the bayonet." "No doubt you could now succeed," was the quiet reply, "but I have one serious objection to your making that attack at this time." "May I ask what that objection is?" was the eager question of the ardent soldier, who saw honor and glory before him in the present opportunity. "I am afraid, sir," rejoined the commander-in-chief, with a mischievous twinkle of his eye which all around enjoyed greatly, "that you would hurt my little friend, Captain———. The enemy left about an hour ago, and he is over there with a [reconnoitering] party."[82]

74. The Best Medicine for Depression

With his army retreating from Petersburg, Lee's only hope of escaping Grant was to secure food for his starved Confederate troops. Lee had planned for the army to rendezvous with hundreds of thousands of rations at Amelia Court House (halfway between Richmond and Appomattox). Yet at Amelia, his hungry men found only a trainload of munitions. One, who saw Lee that day, described him as looking composed, which was normal for Lee; yet, his posture was not as erect as usual. The problems over the last few days had placed "furrows" on his face. The red color of his eyes seemed to prove that he had been crying. His cheeks were "sunken," and his face showed a lack of color. Not a single person who saw him at that time of impending disaster could have forgotten the way he looked.[83]

Even during this sad moment, amounting to almost hopelessness, Lee surrendered to a certain sportive hilarity. What had unexpectedly raised his spirits? One of his generals appeared covered with mud and wrapped in a torn blanket; his face was so smudged with dirt that it presented the appearance "of an Indian painted for" war. When Lee saw him, he roared with laughter.[84]

75. Man's Big Best Friend

A few weeks before Robert E. Lee died, he wrote to his nephew Fitzhugh Lee. "Fitz" had considered giving his uncle a very large pet dog. Part of Lee's letter is an example of both his mirth about the monstrous mutt and his abiding interest in family members. He began his letter by thanking the young man for being considerate of his wishes for a pet. However, he quickly zeroed in on a small problem with the large dog: "I must inform you that it is not my purpose to put my dog to towing canal boats or hauling dirt carts, but I want him to play the part of a friend and protector. His *disposition* is therefore of vital importance—he ought not to be too old to contract a friendship for me—neither is his size so important to me as a perfect form."[85]

76. An Unexcused Absence

Lee had learned during his long military career that sometimes sarcastic humor served as an effective means of gently rebuking those under his command. Later, he used the same technique with students at Washington College. One student, troubled by an unexcused absence, had a meeting with General Lee. The General immediately said that he was happy to see that the lad was now feeling better. Yet, caught off guard, the lad replied that he had been in good health for quite some time. Undeterred, the General then let the lad know that he was glad some good news had finally arrived from home. To which the lad replied: "But General, I have had no bad news." Finally, President Lee struck home: "Ah, I took it for granted that nothing less than sickness or distressing news from home could have kept you from your duty."[86]

77. Worth Her Weight In . . .

Lee, concerned about the costs of maintaining the family home, Arlington plantation, wrote to his son Custis who was legal heir to that property. Lee was partially joking and partially serious when he told his son to "pick up in California some bags of gold, or marry some nice young woman with enough for both." The father wanted his son to gain such independent means that he might hope to "live the life of a country gentleman."[87]

78. "Apples & Chestnuts"

During late 1866, a young set of ladies in Lexington formed a reading club that also included the opposite sex. The group met on Wednesday evenings. One local claimed: "They . . . read a little and talk a great deal." Lee seconded that evaluation by calling the meeting "a great institution for the discussion of apples & chestnuts, but [it] is quite innocent of the pleasures of literature."[88]

79. Do Wrong!

When Lee wanted to impress his officers with the need to obey orders, he told them about General David Twiggs's request to his lieutenants during the Mexican-American War. Lee related that in Mexico, General Twiggs had a unique way of teaching lessons that were extremely effective and never to be forgotten. When Twiggs headed to Mexico, he took with him some young officers who had the habit of not doing what Twiggs had ordered them to do. When Twiggs commented about their attempts to avoid following his orders, these officers were always prepared to demonstrate that "they were right and that" what the General had ordered "was wrong."

General Twiggs was very patient and did not complain or rebuke the officers until one day. That was the day when one of his captains came to report how he had carried out one of General Twiggs's orders. First, the young officer related that he did reach the place where Twiggs had instructed him to go; however, when he was preparing to do what the general had said to do, he found that circumstances were so completely different from what the general had thought that he was sure the general "would not have given" that particular order—if the general had known this new information. So the officer did something else that he thought was best according to the situation. At this point, General Twiggs said: "Captain, I know that you can prove that you are right, and that my order was wrong; in fact, you gentlemen are always right, but for God's sake do wrong sometimes."[89]

80. "Custis Morgan"

"Rare was the animal that did not find favor with Lee, from mouse to rattlesnake." One such animal belonged to his daughter Mildred. The pet was a squirrel named "Custis Morgan." She named him after her brother and the well-known Confederate cavalry commander John Hunt Morgan.[90] Lee worried about this new family member, which he considered too dangerous to be a household pet. He needled the family with a few sarcastic remarks about the squirrel, and he even went so far as to encourage Mildred to prepare a special meal for the family: "Squirrel soup thickened with pea nuts. Custis Morgan in such an exit from the stage would cover himself with glory." True to Lee's concern, before long the four-legged Custis bit Mrs. Lee's doctor. Upon hearing of this attack, Lee again recommended squirrel soup as the cure. Lee was relieved when the little biter went absent without leave and never returned. He felt that the farther away this missing soldier went the better for the family.[91]

81. "Send Me a Kitten"

Stationed in Texas, Lee sent a delightful letter to his youngest daughter Mildred about the animals he saw and lived near. He first informed her that his seven hens, some days, gave him seven eggs. They fed themselves from the corn he gave to the horses. He built a makeshift roost for the hens by using twigs, poles, posts, branches, and the box they came in. He also made sure that their perch was several feet off the ground because of the snakes. Even though he could not protect them from the rain, there was no reason for Mildred to worry because "[s]oldier hens . . . must learn not to mind rain." Switching to another subject, Lee mentioned that he did not have a cat; there were none because wolves had frightened "away all the mice." So he suggested that Mildred send him "a kitten" in her "next letter." He did need a new pet because his only one, a rattlesnake, died one night after becoming sick and refusing to eat his normal meal of frogs.[92]

82. Boy, Girl, Boy . . .

Lee often bantered with his friend Andrew Talcott about their children and future children. The birth of a new Talcott child spawned Lee's congratulatory note. He stated that he was delighted to learn of "the *magnificent* present offered you by Mrs. T. and had some thought of taking the Barge [*sic*] this morning and presenting my congratulations to Mrs. T. in person." He then started to spar with Talcott by making a prediction: "We have been waiting for the event to decide upon the sex of our next and now determine it shall be a girl in order to retain the connection in the family."[93] Lee's prophetic joke later surely got Talcott's attention; true to his prediction, Lee's next child was a girl.

83. Claim It

During the war, Lee tried to respond to most of the letters he received, especially those that were accompanied by a present. His buoyant responses often camouflaged the dour prospects for a Confederate victory. He wrote to Mrs. Roger Pryor that he had found her card, left on the table, at his headquarters the previous night; the card had a hyacinth on it. An inscription on the card stated: "For General Lee, with a kiss." Lee affirmed: "I have my hyacinth and my card and—*I mean to find my kiss!*"[94] Norvell Caskie was one of Lee's special lassies who once sent him a cake. Thanking Norvell, he wrote pointedly: "I prefer kisses to cake."[95] After the war, Lee became acquainted with all of Lexington's children whom he saw during his daily rides. "He could be seen at any time stopping on the streets to kiss some bright-eyed girl, or pass a joke with some sprightly boy."[96]

84. An Amusing Mama's Boy

Several months before Lee left for the United States Military

Academy at West Point, he took classes before noon, and then spent time in the afternoon with his invalid mother. At times, he would arrange to take her on carriage rides into the country. His cousin, Sally Lee remembered how, on one such trip, Robert would begin "doing and saying every thing to amuse" his mother. Once, he provoked loads of laughter by making some paper curtains, which he tried to hang up because his mother had complained about the drafts in the carriage.[97]

85. The Tale He Liked Best

When Lee was growing up, his home contained memorabilia of President George Washington. Lee and his siblings heard stories about how their father, Henry, was so close to Washington that he could even poke fun at the first president. The story Robert E. Lee liked most of all was about the time his father ate dinner with Washington, and the subject of carriage horses was raised. General Washington needed a pair of horses and asked Henry if he knew of any that were available. Henry said that he had two, but that Washington could not have them. The general was curious as to why he could not have the pair. Henry claimed that Washington never gave the full price for any purchase, and that Henry needed all the money he could get. This exchange caused both Mrs. Washington and her pet parrot to start laughing. Washington took the jest in good stride and pointed out: "Ah, Lee, you are a funny fellow. . . . See, that bird is laughing at you."[98]

86. In Good Spirits

Though Lee was not partial to strong drink, he was not overbearing with those who imbibed occasionally, especially during peacetime. Still, he drew a strict line with those who made it a habit of being drunk. "Habitual drunkenness," he claimed, was "*impossible*" for him "to comprehend." Yet, he could joke about those who took a nip every now and then. Once he made a play on words in describing a friend who appeared "badly but was in good *spirits*. His constant companion was a phial of Texas whiskey hermetically sealed to celebrate his meeting with Dick T. [Tilghman] whenever that should take place."[99]

87. Pipe Down!

Robert E. Lee, Jr., recalled:

There is a story told of my father which points to his playful manner. . . . At a certain faculty meeting they were joking Mr. Harris, who so long and so ably filled the chair of Latin, about his walking up the aisle of the Presbyterian church with the stem of his pipe protruding from his pocket. Mr. Harris took out the offending stem and began cutting it shorter. My father, who had been enjoying the incident, said: "No, Mr. Harris, don't do that; next time leave it at home."[100]

88. You Take the High Road, And . . .

Lexington, Virginia, the home of Washington College, was so isolated that it was difficult to travel there from almost anywhere. The closest train happened to be the Chesapeake and Ohio. It stopped regularly at Goshen where passengers started a twenty-three-mile trek. According to David Fleet, these nearly two dozen miles were "the worst and rockyest [sic] roads I ever saw." And the journey took eight hours by stage.

Letters and larger items came "by packet boat" several times each week, or arrived daily by the Staunton stage, traveling on the old Plank Road. There is little doubt why Lee claimed that it made "little difference" which of the two routes one took to Lexington, "for whichever . . . you select, you will wish you had taken the other."[101]

89. Socks You Can Count [On]

Threadbare clothing was fashionable for Confederate soldiers. Those blessed to have shoes also needed socks. So Mrs. Lee and her friends would knit socks and send them to the General for distribution to his men; he would try to give the socks to those troops who were the neediest. Lee often teased Mary because the total number of socks she sent did not always match the total number of the socks she had noted in her accompanying letter.[102]

So he urged her to appoint one of his daughters to make an accurate count. When the next batch of thirty pairs of socks matched the next total of thirty, Lee praised the accomplishment: "I am glad to find there is arithmetic enough in my family to count 30. I thought if you placed your daughter at work all would go right."[103]

90. Love Affairs

According to Robert E. Lee, Jr.:

My father was always greatly interested in the love affairs of his relatives, friends, and acquaintances. His letters during the war show this in very many ways. One would suppose that the general commanding an army in active operations could not find the time even to think of such trifles, much less to write about them; but he knew of very many such affairs among his officers and even his men, and would on occasion refer to them before the parties themselves, very much to their surprise and discomfiture. Bishop Peterkin, of West Virginia, who served on the staff of General Pendleton, tells me of the following instances, in illustration of this characteristic:

It was in the winter of 1863-4, when we were camped near Orange Court House, [upon] meeting the General after I had come back from a short visit to Richmond, he asked after my father, and then said, "Did you see Miss——?" and I replied, "No, sir; I did not." Then again, "Did you see Miss——?" and when I still replied "No," he added, with a smile, "How exceedingly busy you must have been." Again at the cavalry review at Brandy Station, on June 8, 1863[,] we had galloped all around the lines, when the General took his post for the "march past," and all the staff in attendance grouped themselves about him. There being no special orders about our positions, I got pretty near the

General. I noticed that several times he turned and looked toward an ambulance near us, filled with young girls. At last, after regiments and brigades had gone by, the Horse Artillery came up. The General turned and, finding me near him said, "Go and tell that young lady with the blue ribbon in her hat that such-and-such a battery is coming." I rode up and saluted the young lady. There was great surprise shown by the entire party, as I was not known to any of them, and when I came out with my message there was a universal shout, while the General looked on with a merry twinkle in his eye. It was evidently the following up on his part of some joke which he had with the young lady about an officer in this battery.[104]

91. Robert Who?

When Lee returned home from the Mexican-American War, he saw an attractive little lad whose hair sported a curl. Lee, sensing that the child was his own son, Robert, Jr., asked sprightly: "Where's my little boy?" He then proceeded to lift the child into the air joyously. Yet, he soon learned to his embarrassment that the child in his arms was a visitor, Armistead Lippitt.[105]

92. No Vacancy

When the Lees lived in Baltimore, they often had enough visitors to fill their Madison Avenue row house. In April 1851, Lee returned to Baltimore after visiting his son Custis, a cadet at West Point. Arriving early that morning, he was unaware that his wife had invited her Randolph clan to stay. He entered the house, went to the second floor, and knocked gently on his bedroom door. Mrs. Lee immediately came to the door and quietly told him that Emma Randolph was in her bed. Lee then tried his daughter Mary's room where he found cousin Cornelia Randolph sleeping. To boot, Robert, Jr., and Mildred were sleeping with their brother Fitzhugh (called Rooney). Lee recalled: "I did not venture to examine farther into the house. . . . After a reasonable time we all assembled at the breakfast table & laughed over the adventures of the morning."[106]

93. A Spell

The nation's condition looked bleak just before Virginia's secession. And Lee knew that the day might soon arrive when he would have to make a momentous decision.

According to Margaret Sanborn, Lee was able to put such problems out of his mind and keep his composure. What diversions helped him to pass these worrisome days? He played with his new grandson, chatted with visiting friends, and wrote letters. He wrote to Mildred lively and humorous descriptions of the family's pets. The new dog, he claimed, was always waging war with cats and even taking on the appearance of a "veteran." Lee worried about Tom the cat; he was afraid that Tom would be spoiled by one of Lee's daughters who wanted to clothe the four-legged warrior in "ruffles." Lee feared that such a uniform might curb Tom's pursuit of mice. "Your sisters never array him in collars, believing that beauty unadorned is adorned the most, & that they would cloud his verdant eyes." Lee also jested with Mildred: "I noticed that you spelt Saturday with two ts (Satturday). One is considered enough in the Army, but perhaps the fashion is two."[107]

94. Making Mary Jealous?

According to author John Perry, in the early 1830s Lee would write to his wife that he flirted with other women while she was gone.[108] Once he wrote that he had been walking with two ladies at one time, and he told Mary that if she did not hurry to join him, he might become another woman's boyfriend. He recalled this event: "How I did strut along with one hand on my whiskers & the other elevating my coat tail! . . . Surely that was a sight for Old Pointers to see."[109] In Baltimore, during the early 1850s, Lee was very conscious of his attire though Mary cared little about fashion. So he picked on her by asking why she did not wear longer dresses; then he wrote that if she did not do so, he would go walking with those who did.[110]

A few years later while in San Antonio, Texas, he wrote to his wife that he had been invited to a gathering at a young widow's house; however he did not go. Later he thought that it would be courteous to make an appearance. So he located the house that evening, went in, and was as patient as he could be for a few minutes. Then as he was preparing to leave, the widow offered to take him outside to see her crops. "But she had waked the wrong passenger. I told her I had no knowledge of horticulture, and took no interest in agriculture in Texas."[111]

95. Blood Always Thicker Than Water?

Lee was only partially jesting when he wrote to daughter Mary about his nephew, Louis Marshall (the son of Lee's sister in Baltimore). Louis was fighting alongside Union general John Pope at that time. In his note, Lee informed little Mary that Robert, Jr., was with Stonewall Jackson, and "I hope [Jackson] will catch Pope and [your cousin] Louis. . . . I could forgive the latter for fighting against us, if he had not joined such a miscreant as Pope."[112]

96. Laughter in the Night

Lee had scarcely fallen asleep when Captain Powers Smith arrived after a reconnaissance. Sitting up to greet the messenger, Lee said: "Ah, Captain, you have returned, have you?" Lee beckoned Smith to come sit beside him and share any new information. According to Captain Smith, when he sat beside Lee, the General acted in a fatherly manner by wrapping his arm around Smith and pulling him close. Having heard the young man's report, Lee began to jest with him. While Smith was leaving, Lee was still having friendly conversation with officers bedded down nearby. As Smith rode away from Lee's headquarters, he still heard the General's "hearty laughter . . . again and again."[113]

97. Don't Become a Soldier

Lee could not encourage aspiring young men to pursue a military career. Before the war, he wrote to his wife's cousin that he could not advise any young person to go into the army. He noted that the same effort, self-denial, and stamina used in other fields of endeavor would bring much more success and bring it more quickly.[114]

When one of his sons, William H. Fitzhugh (called Rooney), dropped out of college and secured a commission (with the help of Lee's superior, General Winfield Scott), Lee sent the general a sporting thank-you note: "[A]s you (used to) say, 'boys are only fit to be shot' & [since Rooney] seems to have had from infancy an ardent desire for this high privilege, perhaps the sooner it is done the better."[115]

98. Animal Sacrifice

Not long after the battle of Fredericksburg, Lee started leaving his tent flap open for one particular female, a camp follower who regularly hid under his cot.

[A]mong a number of fowls presented to the general was a sprightly hen, who went into the egg business [for a while. General Lee] . . . persuaded Bryan[, his] well-known steward, that her egg, which she each morning deposited in the general's tent, was better for the general's breakfast than herself. Lee, fond of domestic animals, appreciated her selection of his quarters, and would leave the tent door open for her and wait elsewhere until her cackle informed him that he could return to his canvas home. She roosted and rode in his wagon, was an eye-witness of the battle of Chancellorsville, and there it is said she refused to lay until victory perched upon her general's plume, when she at once commenced. Many months she soldiered—participated, in her way, in the battle of Gettysburg, but when the orders were given to fall back, and the headquarters wagons had been loaded, the hen could not be found. General Lee joined others in a search for her, and finally she was found perched on top of the wagon seemingly anxious to return to her native State. In the fall of 1864, when Lee's headquarters were [*sic*] near Orange Court House, the hen had become fat and lazy, and on one occasion when the general had a distinguished visitor to dine with him, Bryan, finding it difficult to procure suitable material, unknown to every one, killed the hen. At dinner the general was surprised to see so fine a fowl, and all enjoyed it, not dreaming of the great sacrifice made upon the altar of hospitality.[116]

99. They'll Think You Are Crazy

Lee was stationed in New York when his wife arrived in 1841 to fix up their house at Fort Hamilton in Brooklyn. For most New Yorkers, Mary Lee's use of servants, to help maintain the house and take care of her small children, was a totally new concept. Her husband even poked fun at her and warned that the neighbors seemed "to have some misgivings as to whether you possess all your faculties." At Arlington plantation, however, Mary had been in the midst of slaves since her birth. So she felt that they were needed to maintain the house and the family, especially since her health was delicate, and five children needed tending. Yet, after Lee's banter subsided, he was in agreement that she needed the servants.[117]

100. Ruler of the Roost

Lee's lampooning, directed toward his family, was sometimes sarcastic. He gave the following evaluation of his youngest unmarried daughter: "[Mildred] rules her brother and my nephews with an iron rod, and scatters her advice broadcast among the young men of the College. . . . The young mothers of Lexington ought to be extremely grateful to her for her suggestions to them as to the proper mode of rearing their children."[118]

101. Courting Rules

If gentlemen callers overstayed their visits with his daughters, Lee employed a unique way of razzing them. When the young men came to the Lee house, General Lee's daughters took them into the parlor and closed the door; then the General and Mrs. Lee occupied a nearby dining room. At ten o'clock sharp, the General entered the parlor and started to close the shutters.

With his entry, most visitors immediately bid farewell. Yet when some callers were slow to respond to this family routine, Lee remonstrated strongly: "Good night, young gentlemen." If this failed to get their attention, the General took his daughters' place for a conversation with the young men. For even the most recalcitrant callers, the idea of having to talk with General Lee, after spending an evening with his daughters, proved too much; the young men soon went their way.[119]

102. Fun on Horseback

When Mildred Lee was at home, she and her father would go on horseback rides. On those joyful occasions, the General's posture was straight, and he appeared "dignified" astride Traveller. Mildred, on Lucy Long, did her best to stay abreast of the General. He often took off joyfully and raced Traveller far ahead to a hill and there waited for his trailing daughter. She thought that these rides rested him more than anything else. "If I were silent he would say 'Life[,] tell me something—tell me about those schoolmates whom [*sic*] Rob says have experienced every calamity but matrimony.'"[120]

103. The Old General Husband

During the 1840s Lee poked fun about the marriage of an old general. His name was Edmund Pendleton Gaines, and the irony was that he had married a very young widow; the general was seventy years of age. Lee wrote: "She declares that the Genl. has more than fulfilled every promise he ever made her, . . . [and] her prospects are very good of again becoming a happy widow."[121]

104. Contagious Laughter

In Lee's youth, he was often surrounded by women. Author Margaret Sanborn believes this female companionship helped him to develop a talent for conversation. That is why women often appreciated his presence. She also believes that he learned how to tell stories from his father, which helped him fit in with groups of men. One friend wrote of Lee's "sparkling conversation and lively stories" which he claimed could make Lee's listeners "'laugh very heartily' while Robert himself laughed 'until the tears ran down his face.'"[122]

105. "Rejoicings of the Saints"

At times, Lee's humor strongly caricatured the enemy. During April 1863, he enjoyed the antics of Union general Joseph Hooker and perceived them to be more of an irritant than a threat. He reported that the enemy was very active in trying to trick him. The week before, they had bristled around the riverbanks, and then suddenly disappeared. Next, they formed a battle line, including skirmishers, cannon, and support vehicles. After dark they built fires and cut wood until midnight, and then vanished. Lee was passionate the next day when he noted their more outrageous escapades: "[A] party crossed at Port Royal in their pontoon boats, stole from our citizens all they could get and recrossed before we could get them. Their expeditions will serve as texts to the writers of the *Herald, Tribune & Times* for brilliant accounts of grand Union victories & great rejoicings of the saints of the [Republican] party."[123]

106. The Horseless Carriage

Lee would tease his troops, especially those who needed "a little loosening up." On one occasion, Jeb Stuart's staff member Major Heros "German Goliath" von Borcke purchased a carriage so that he could have the horses that came with it. The frugal von Borcke wanted to use the carriage as a military "baggage wagon." This brought out the best humor in Lee; and, thereafter, he hardly ever passed von Borcke that he did not mention the carriage. During a small fight, von Borcke was with Lee. This gave Lee a chance to needle the German: "If we only had your carriage, what a splendid opportunity to charge the enemy with it."[124]

107. Borrow Her Back

In August 1863, with a daughter-in-law in poor health and a son perpetually postponing his engagement, General Lee advised Mrs.

Lee: "You have no immediate prospects of acquiring any new daughters . . . [For this reason] you must take good care of your old ones." He then told her he had pains in his back and hoped that he could spread those medicines, recommended by his doctors, on the backs of other family members. He noted: "I wish I had [daughter Mary's] back here to apply it to, it might do it service."[125]

108. Chimneys

A humorous Lee statement could present itself at almost any time. During a tense retreat, with supplies running short, General Lee was searching his map for a spot named Stone Chimneys. One "young officer" was certain that they had already reached Stone Chimneys because he could recall vividly when the chimneys had been built. Lee listened with glee at the officer's recollection, and he then scorched him by saying: "[I]f you remember when the chimneys were built, this is not the place. The stone chimneys mentioned on this map were built before you were."[126]

109. Claim that Kiss Later

In the tense days leading to Virginia's secession from the Union, Lee sent in his resignation from President Abraham Lincoln's army on a Saturday. (Although Lee was unaware of it that morning, he would soon be commanding all of Virginia's forces.) The next day, he and his daughter went to church. After leaving the service, Lee lingered outside for a discussion with several strangers; his daughter went to her cousin's house nearby to await her father. Lee's conversation lasted so long that his daughter, sitting at the second-floor window watching the meeting in the street below, became restless. She was absorbed by the "suspense and uncertainty" of exactly what her father and these men were talking about. At last, Lee came to the door of the cousin's house; then, in a lighthearted way requested a kiss from the "young hostess." To his surprise, she refused—she would not give him a kiss unless he pledged "to take command" of Virginia's defenses. He replied that he could not make such a promise. Why?

Because no one had made him an official offer; then he and his daughter left. That night, Lee received a request from

Virginia's governor to meet with him in Richmond the next day. Yet, the governor's message did not state the purpose of the meeting. Still, the next morning, as Lee passed through Alexandria on his way to Richmond, he felt enough assurance about what would occur later that day that he returned to the cousin's house to "claim that kiss."[127]

110. Agnes

According to Lee's son Robert, Jr.:

About the first week of November [1865] we all went by canal-boat to "Bremo" . . . where we remained the guests of Doctor and Mrs. Charles Cocke until we went to Lexington. My sister Agnes, while there, was invited to Richmond to assist at the wedding of a very dear friend, Miss Sally Warwick. She wrote to my father asking his advice and approval, and received this reply, so characteristic of his playful, humorous mood:

"My Precious Little Agnes: I have just received your letter of the 13th and hasten to reply. It is very hard for you to apply to me to advise you to go away from me. You know how much I want to see you, and how important you are to me. But in order to help you to make up your mind, if it will promote your pleasure and Sally's happiness, I will say go. You may inform Sally from me, however, that no preparations are necessary, and if they were[,] no one could help her. She has just got to wade through it as if it was an attack of measles or anything else naturally. As she would not marry [my son] Custis, she may marry whom she chooses. I shall wish her every happiness, just the same, for she knows nobody loves her as much as I do. I do not think, upon reflection, she will consider it right to refuse my son and take away my daughter. She need not tell me whom she is going to marry. I suppose it is some cross old widower, with a dozen children. She will not be satisfied at her sacrifice with less, and I should think that would be cross sufficient. I hope [your sister] 'Life' is not going to desert us too, and when are we to see you?"[128]

111. Keep Off the Grass!

Robert, Jr., recollected:

My father . . . as I have said before, commenced almost as soon as he became president of the college to improve the grounds, roads, walks, fences, etc., and systematically kept this work up to the time of his death. The walks about the college grounds were in a very bad condition, and, in wet weather, often ankle deep in mud. As a first step toward improving them the president had a quantity of limestone broken up and spread upon the roads and walks. The rough, jagged surface was most uninviting, and horsemen and footmen naturally took to the grass. Seeing Colonel T. L. Preston riding one day across the campus on his way to his classes at the Virginia Military Institute, my father remarked: "Ah, Colonel, I have depended upon you and your big sorrel to help smooth down my walks!" Another day, a student who was walking on the grass saw the General not far away, and immediately stepped into the middle of the rocks, upon which he manfully trudged along. A strange lady, going in the same direction, followed in the student's footsteps, and when the youth came within speaking distance, my father, with a twinkle in his eye, thanked him for setting so good an example, and added, "The ladies do not generally take kindly to my walks."[129]

112. Mercy on the Bachelor

Lee cut up with his daughter about the bachelorhood of her brother Robert, Jr. Lee wrote on March 28, 1868:

My Precious Agnes: I was so glad to receive your letter, to learn that you were well and enjoying yourself among pleasant friends. I hope that you will soon get through all your visits and come home. Your uncle Smith says you girls ought to marry his sons, as you both find it so agreeable to be from home, and you could then live a true Bohemian life and have a happy time generally. But I do not agree with him; I shall not give my consent, so you must choose elsewhere. . . . Fitzhugh writes that everything is blooming at the "White

House," and his wheat is splendid. I am in hopes that it is all due to the presence of my fair daughter. Rob says that things at Romancoke are not so prosperous[;] you see, there is no Mrs. R. E. Lee, Jr., there, and that may make a difference. Cannot you persuade some of those pretty girls in Baltimore to take compassion on a poor bachelor?[130]

113. Inspection

When Lee was stationed at Fort Monroe in early 1834, General John Ellis Wool, inspector general of the army, came to examine the fortifications. Lee was not in the best mood due to a quarrel among the troops. So Lee's sarcasm was ripe when he wrote about this inspection. He asked General Wool to begin the inspection at once so that the troops could receive their "measure of *Glory* for the week." After the first part of the inspection took place, Lee claimed that the general's "Punctilio" was apparently satisfied and that the general had "postponed his annihilation" of the rest of the fortifications until early the following morning. To Lee's chagrin, the inspector even asked if it were not possible for Lee and others to live outside the fort, which probably further agitated Lee.[131]

114. "You'll Fit Right In"

The Lee girls, like most wartime Confederate women, wore simple clothes. When Lee's daughter Mildred wrote of her skimpy wardrobe, he chuckled in response, "[P]oor little [Mildred's] wardrobe." He offered her socks and a pair of boots. However, most of all he felt that she would be inconspicuous at his camp. There, near Fredericksburg, he wrote that his troops were "accustomed to short commons every way & scant wardrobes are fashionable."[132]

115. Salamanders

During his last year with the United States military, Lee wrote from Texas that, at times, San Antonio was so hot he had to go swimming to get relief from the heat. He wrote to his daughter Agnes: "The thermometer has been ranging up to a hundred degrees for nearly three weeks, occasionally exceeding it. . . . If any of your friends are preparing to personate [*sic*] salamanders, send them out."[133]

116. Breakfast Menus

Near the end of the war and shortly before Lee had to abandon Petersburg, his army was starving. So he cut through the tension of the times in a conversation about food with General John B. Gordon. Lee told Gordon about a recent message that General Grant had sent during a cease-fire to bury the dead. The Union general claimed that he watched Lee so closely that he knew what Lee ate for breakfast each day. Lee continued:

I told that officer [who brought this information] to tell General Grant that I thought there must be some mistake about the latter message, for unless [General Grant] had fallen from grace since I last saw him, he would not permit me to eat such a breakfast as mine without dividing his with me. I also requested that officer to present my compliments to General Grant, and say to him that I knew perhaps as much about his dinners as he knew about my breakfasts.[134]

117. Rags

The lighthearted and tender manner that Lee displayed toward his wife was often mixed with gaiety and jest. One day when he was walking back and forth across the room, his wife was conversing with a student who had fought in the war. Their conversation centered upon the great difference between the well-dressed Union soldiers and the ragged Confederates. This point obviously grabbed Lee's attention; his eyes opened wide, and, when Mrs. Lee had finished, he gracefully interjected: "But, ah! Mistress Lee, we gave them some awful hard knocks, [even] with all our rags."[135]

118. "My Order Was Not for You"

In 1864, when a campaign was about to begin, an order was given for "Women" to go "to the rear." Yet, since Union soldiers did not seem to be eager to move against Lee's troops, some of his officers' wives remained nearby. When Lee boarded the train at Orange Court House, he saw Captain A. R. H. Ranson and wife. Lee stopped to ask the captain to introduce his wife to him. She quickly apologized for not heeding Lee's order and claimed she was the transgressor, not her husband. Then, she asked his forgiveness. Lee tried to calm her fears by explaining that his order had not been for her; it had been for Captain Ranson. Lee was planning get a lot of work out of her husband that summer, he explained, and he could not do it if the Captain's horse was not rested. Lee said that each night he saw Captain Ranson leaving for Orange Court House, some three miles distant. Then each morning, he saw him returning. Lee felt that this was too much for the horse. So he intended to put a stop to it. Lee then seated himself by Mrs. Ranson and put her at ease with genial conversation. Even though she was glad to have experienced Lee's geniality and kindness rather than his sternness and rebuke, she was keenly aware that he had been watching her husband very closely.[136]

119. Pikes, Anyone?

One Confederate general in Kentucky complained that he needed more modern arms and equipment to fight against the Union forces there. Lee responded that he had no modern arms to send; however, he promised the general that he could send him some "pikes."[137]

120. Rainy Retreat

During its retreat from Gettysburg, Lee's Army of Northern Virginia faced an unexpected obstacle near Hagerstown, Maryland—the suddenly rising waters of the Potomac River. Intense rains swelled the river, crippling Lee's attempt to cross into Virginia's safety. Had Lee's army been trapped by the river, it might have faced disaster at the hand of General George

Gordon Meade's trailing forces. Though the large rain had been a surprise, Lee's humor, even in the face of potential doom, was not. With one of his lieutenants, the stoic Lee jovially asked, "Does it ever quit raining about here? If so, I should like to see a clear day."[138]

121. John Brown

Lee's levity could pop up unexpectedly even in the face of execution. In 1859, then-Lieutenant Colonel Robert E. Lee, along with Jeb Stuart and a group of U. S. Marines, bagged John Brown and his band of insurrectionists at Harper's Ferry, which was then a part of Virginia. Brown was soon tried, convicted, and sentenced to be hanged for this crime. Since the whole nation had been aroused by Brown's attack on Harper's Ferry, Lee, with several military companies, had returned to Harper's Ferry to insure a peaceful execution. While Brown was preparing to die on the gallows the next day, Lee was writing to his wife about the situation; he even inserted a brief side message to his handsome brother Smith Lee:

> To-morrow [*sic*] will probably see the last of Captain Brown. . . .
> There will be less interest for the others [captured with him],
> but still I think the troops will not be withdrawn till they are
> similarly disposed of. This morning I was introduced to Mrs.
> Brown, who with a Mr. Tyndale and Mrs. McKim, all from
> Philadelphia, has come on to have a last interview with her husband. As it is a matter over which I have no control, and wish
> to take none, I referred them to General William B. Taliaferro
> [commanding Virginia's troops]. Tell Smith that no charming
> women have insisted on taking charge of me, as they are always
> doing of him. I am [thus] left to my own resources.[139]

122. Apple Tree Diplomacy

Just before Lee surrendered to Grant at Appomattox, Virginia, Lee's headquarters had been in the midst of a group of nearby trees. For this reason a false rumor started that the surrender took place under an apple tree. So, not long after the war, Lee was asked if he and Grant had held their meeting under that tree. Lee explained: "We met in Mr. McLean's parlor. If there was an apple tree there, I did not see it!"[140]

123. Moss Neck Neckin'

During the war . . .

Captain Smith tells another anecdote. . . . When [a Union general], crossed the Rappahannock [River] below Fredericksburg[, Virginia], Captain Smith was sent to tell General Lee of it. He found no one stirring at headquarters except Colonel Venerable, who was washing his face in a basin on a stump, and told him that the General was asleep in his tent, but that he had better go in at once and wake him. The Captain found the great Chieftain sleeping so sweetly that he hesitated for a minute to awaken him, but finally called him and he arose and asked what was wanted. The young aid replied that he had some very important information that the enemy had crossed the river.

"Well, come and sit on the side of my couch, and tell me all about it," Lee said with his usual kindly smile.

After listening to the details the General said, "you are sure that the enemy has crossed the river? I did not know but that a certain colonel on your staff had heard firing in the direction of Moss Neck, and had gone down there on a reconnoitering expedition."

The pleasant allusion was to Col. A. S. Pendleton, of [Stonewall] Jackson's staff, who was then paying devoted attention to Miss Corbin of Moss Neck, whom he married not long afterwards.

General Lee then reflected for a few minutes and said, "Well, you wish me to give you some message for your General, do you not? Tell General Jackson that he knows as well what to do with the enemy as I do. Tell him to dispose of them as he finds best, and I will come down after a while to see how he is getting along." And with other kind words and good wishes for his young friend, Lee dismissed him, and Captain Smith galloped back to tell Jackson what Lee had said.[141]

124. A Lesson about Crows

Robert, Jr., told of a lesson he learned from his good-natured father:

I was given a gun of my own and allowed to go shooting by myself. My father, to give me an incentive, offered a reward for every crow-scalp I could bring him, and, in order that I might get to work at once, advanced a small sum with which to buy powder and shot, this sum to be returned to him out of the first scalps obtained. My industry and zeal were great, my hopes high, and by good luck I did succeed in bagging two crows about the second time I went out. I showed them with great pride to my father, intimating that I should short-ly be able to return him his loan, and that he must be pre-pared to hand over to me very soon further rewards for my skill. His eyes twinkled and his smile showed that he had strong doubts about my making an income by killing crows, and he was right, for I never killed another, though I tried hard and long.[142]

125. Hurry Up and Snooze!

Robert, Jr., allowed:

My father was the most punctual man I ever knew. He was always ready for family prayers, for meals, and met every engagement, social or business, at the moment. He expect-ed all of us to be the same, and taught us the use and neces-sity of forming such habits for the convenience of all concerned. I never knew him [to be] late for Sunday service at the Post Chapel. He used to appear some minutes before the rest of us, in uniform, jokingly rallying my mother for being late, and for forgetting something at the last moment.

When he could wait no longer for her, he would say that he was off and would march along to church by himself, or with any of the children who were ready. There he sat, very straight well up the middle aisle and, as I remember, always became very sleepy, and sometimes even took a little nap during the sermon. At that time, this drowsiness of my father's was something awful to me, inexplicable. I know it was hard for me to keep awake, and frequently I did not; but why he, who to my mind could do everything that was right, without any effort, should sometimes be overcome, I could not understand, and did not try to do so.[143]

Notes
Abbreviations

Coulling—Mary P. Coulling, *The Lee Girls* (Winston-Salem, North Carolina: John F. Blair Pub., 1987).

Dowdey—Clifford Dowdey, *Lee* (Boston: Little, Brown, 1965).

Wartime—Clifford Dowdey and Louis H. Manarin, eds. *The Wartime Papers of R. E. Lee* (Boston: Little, Brown, 1961).

The Encyclopedia Americana—*The Encyclopedia Americana Complete in Thirty Volumes* (New York: Americana Corporation, 1951).

Fellman—Michael Fellman, *The Making of Robert E. Lee* (New York: Random House, 2000).

Fishwick—Marshall W. Fishwick, *Lee after the War* (New York: Dodd, Mead, 1963).

Flood—Charles Bracelen Flood, *Lee: The Last Years* (Boston: Houghton Mifflin, 1981).

LLI—Douglas Southall Freeman, *Lee's Lieutenants: A Study in Command,* vol. 1 (New York: Charles Scribner's Sons, 1943).

FI—Douglas Southall Freeman, *R. E. Lee: A Biography,* vol. 1 (New York: Charles Scribner's Sons, 1942).

FII—Douglas Southall Freeman, *R. E. Lee: A Biography,* vol. 2 (New York: Charles Scribner's Sons, 1937).

FIII—Douglas Southall Freeman, *R. E. Lee: A Biography,* vol. 3 (New York: Charles Scribner's Sons, 1937).

FIV—Douglas Southall Freeman, *R. E. Lee: A Biography,* vol. 4 (New York: Charles Scribner's Sons, 1946).

Gallagher, *Fighting*—Gary W. Gallagher, ed. *Fighting for the Confederacy: The Personal Recollections of General Edward Porter Alexander* (Chapel Hill: The University of North Carolina Press, 1989).

Gerson—Noel B. Gerson, *Light-Horse Harry, A Biography of Washington's Great Cavalryman, General Henry Lee* (Garden City, New York: Doubleday & Co., 1966).

Gignilliat—John L. Gignilliat, "A Historian's Dilemma: A Posthumous Footnote for Freeman's R. E. Lee," *The Journal of Southern History,* 43, May 1977.

Johnson—William J. Johnson, *Robert E. Lee: The Christian* (Reprint. Arlington Heights, Illinois: Christian Liberty Press, n.d.).

L&L—Rev. J. William Jones, DD. *Life and Letters of Robert Edward Lee, Soldier and Man* (Reprint. Harrisonburg, Virginia: Sprinkle Publications, 1986).

Rem—Rev. J. William Jones, DD. *Personal Reminiscences of Gen. Robert E. Lee* (New York: D. Appleton, 1875).

Fitzhugh Lee—Fitzhugh Lee, *General Lee: A Biography of Robert E. Lee* (Reprint. New York: De Capo Press, 1994).

Rec—Capt. Robert E. Lee, *Recollections and Letters of General Robert E. Lee* (Reprint. New York: Garden City Pub., 1924).

Mason—Emily V. Mason, *Popular Life of Gen. Robert Edward Lee* (Baltimore: John Murphy & Co., 1872).

McCaslin—Richard B. McCaslin, *Lee in the Shadow of Washington* (Baton Rouge: Louisiana State University Press, 2001).

LA—John Perry, *Lady of Arlington: The Life of Mrs. Robert E. Lee* (Sisters, Oregon: Multnomah Pub., 2001).

SI—Margaret Sanborn, *Robert E. Lee,* vol. 1 (Philadelphia: J. B. Lippincott, 1966).

SII—Margaret Sanborn, *Robert E. Lee,* vol. 2 (Philadelphia: J. B. Lippincott, 1967).

Taylor, *Duty*—John M. Taylor, *Duty Faithfully Performed: Robert E. Lee and His Critics* (Dulles, Virginia: Brassey's, 1999).

Trudeau—Noah Andre Trudeau, *Gettysburg: A Testing of Courage* (New York: Harper Collins Pub., 2002).

Wiencek—Henry Wiencek, *An Imperfect God: George Washington, His Slaves, and the Creation of America* (New York: Farrar, Straus and Giroux, 2003).

Wilkins—J. Steven Wilkins, *Call of Duty: The Sterling Nobility of Robert E. Lee* (Nashville, Tennessee: Cumberland House Pub., 1997).

The World Book Encyclopedia—*The World Book Encyclopedia* (Chicago: World Book, Inc., 1988).

1. Rev. J. William Jones, DD, *Life and Letters of Robert Edward Lee, Soldier and Man* (Reprint. Harrisonburg, Virginia: Sprinkle Publications, 1986), pp. 151-52.

About the same time, Lee wrote to his wife Mary. His sarcasm was obvious when he stated: "I am sorry . . . that the movements of the armies cannot keep pace with the expectations of the editors of the papers"(Margaret Sanborn, *Robert E. Lee*, vol. 2, Philadelphia: J. B. Lippincott, 1967, p. 27). After the war, two Tennesseans at Washington College overheard Lee tell a visitor that General Nathan Bedford Forrest "accomplished more with fewer troops than any other officer on either side" (Charles Bracelen Flood, *Lee: The Last Years*, Boston: Houghton Mifflin, 1981, p. 146).

2. Douglas Southall Freeman, *R. E. Lee: A Biography*, vol. 1 (New York: Charles Scribner's Sons, 1942), p. 297.

After examining Mary Custis Lee's journal, author John Perry noted her hesitation to marry Robert E. Lee because she questioned his commitment to Jesus Christ. Mary felt that his "faith was superficial and incomplete" even though his mother had passed on her strong biblical foundation to the children. Lee had been raised in church and had been taught his church "catechism" before he could read; still, his future wife was concerned about the "depth and sincerity" of his faith. Regardless of his involvement in church, he had never spoken of a "personal relationship with Christ." Though she had long maintained an abiding affection for him, Mary was still uncertain if she should become his wife (John Perry, *Lady of Arlington: The Life of Mrs. Robert E. Lee*, Sisters, Oregon: Multnomah Pub., 2001, pp. 73-74). Regardless, in 1831 she married Lee, a lifelong Episcopalian.

In 1849, after Lee heard a particular sermon, he noted that he was very sensitive to the sins mentioned in that sermon but found it hard to conduct himself properly.

> Man's nature is so selfish, so weak, every feeling & every passion urging him to folly, excess & sin [so] that I am disgusted with myself & sometimes with all the world. . . . Even in my progress, I fail, & my only hope is in my confidence, my trust in the mercy of God which is deep and unbounded (Michael Fellman, *The Making of Robert E. Lee*, New York: Random House, 2000, p. 50).

According to author Michael Fellman, on July 17, 1853, upon certainty that he had come to salvation through Christ, Lee was confirmed in Alexandria, Virginia (ibid., p. 51). Lee lightheartedly described "Episcopalians" to one of his daughters in December 1866:

This is the night for the supper for the repairs to the Episcopal church. Your mother and sisters are busy with their contributions. It is to take place at the hotel, and your brother, cousins, and father are to attend. On Monday night (24th), the supper for the Presbyterian church is to be held at their lecture-room. They are to have music and every attraction. I hope both may be productive of good. But you know the Episcopalians are few in numbers and light in purse, and must be resigned to small returns. (Capt. Robert E. Lee, *Recollections and Letters of General Robert E. Lee,* reprint, New York: Garden City Pub., 1924, p. 248).

3. Ralston B. Lattimore, ed., *The Story of Robert E. Lee as told in his own words and those of his contemporaries,* Source Book Series, No. 1 (Philadelphia: Eastern National Park & Monument Association, 1964), pp. 86-87.

Robert E. Lee accepted the presidency of Washington College at the end of August 1865 and served in that capacity until he died in October 1870. Graham's confession may have reminded Lee of his own father, Henry "Light-Horse Harry" Lee. As a teenager at Princeton, Henry laughed loudly when a prankster set off "a charge of gunpowder . . . in [a] room" (Noel B. Gerson, *Light-Horse Harry, A Biography of Washington's Great Cavalryman, General Henry Lee,* Garden City, New York: Doubleday & Co., 1966., pp. 11-12).

In the 1820s, Robert E. Lee was attending the United States Military Academy at West Point, New York, where he was normally hardworking and diligent in his studies. Yet, like all cadets, Lee probably had to fight against temptations to break academy regulations. He was not one to hang around bored, but enjoyed an innocent good time with fellow cadets. And he was not a stranger to a joke or a tease. Just like his father, Lee enjoyed an occasional practical joke, such as knocking on doors (then hurrying off before an answer), leaving unsigned messages, or even eyeing attractive girls with a telescope. Yet, he diligently ensured that his antics remained within the bounds of school policy (SI, p. 60).

4. Rev. J. William Jones, DD, *Personal Reminiscences of Gen. Robert E. Lee* (New York: D. Appleton, 1875), pp. 165-66.

Lee's father, Henry "Light-Horse Harry" Lee, was a famed cavalry commander during the American Revolution. Henry (or

Harry) taught his very young son Robert riding, prizing intellectual pursuits, seeking a place in the military, and placing "a higher value on personal integrity and moral courage than on life itself" (Gerson, p. 223). Harry Lee, regularly in debt after the war, went to debtor's prison; during his incarceration he wrote a book about his wartime experiences. One of Harry's fears was that he might be sued for libel (ibid., p. 227). Harry's longtime friend, President James Madison, once challenged a young Robert E. Lee: "Let your father's honor and matchless gallantry set an example that you will never forget" (ibid., p. 237). Robert could not have known his father well since Harry went to the West Indies during the War of 1812; he died on the return trip in 1818 and was buried in Georgia.

5. Rec, pp. 315-16.

6. FI, p. 190. Lee sported a moustache during his latter years in the United States military. However, by October 1861, he bore a full beard that startled some of his old friends. When he came back to Richmond, one of them, a Miss Pegram, did not like his changed appearance. Lee chuckled: "Why, you would not have a soldier in the field to look rough, would you? There is little time there for shaving and personal adornment" (FI, p. 577, footnote 78).

Arlington—This was the large plantation owned by Robert E. Lee's father-in-law, George Washington Parke Custis, the adopted son of George Washington (LA, p. 27).

Lee's wife and her children were raised there. When Mr. Custis died, Lee's son Custis inherited the property. The Lees had to abandon Arlington shortly before the major hostilities of 1861. During the war, the plantation was seized by the Federal government; later, it was used as a military cemetery, and for a while it became a refuge for former slaves. After Lee's death, a court battle ensued between the Federal government and his son Custis over the plantation's legal ownership. In the early 1880s, Custis won the case. The high court judged that the Federal government had acted illegally in seizing and retaining the property. Custis sold Arlington to the government for $150,000 (Mary P. Coulling, *The Lee Girls*, Winston-Salem, North Carolina: John F. Blair Pub., 1987, p. 186).

Today, Arlington is America's most hallowed military cemetery. In 1925, Congress designated the large mansion there as "the Lee Mansion National Memorial" and by 1955 it was "officially named the Robert E. Lee Memorial" (LA, p. 345).

7. Rec, pp. 9-10. Lee was fond of having his hands and his feet

tickled. During his last two weeks: Lee's bed was brought down to the first floor; doctors labored over him; it rained heavily; and his daughter Agnes rubbed his hands, as she had years before at Arlington (Coulling, p. 175). When he died a few days later, Agnes chose to bury him in his "black broadcloth suit" (ibid., p. 176). She had wanted to dress the body in his Confederate uniform but was afraid to do so because she feared the possible charge of treason (ibid., p. 177).

8. Emily V. Mason, *Popular Life of Gen. Robert Edward Lee* (Baltimore: John Murphy & Co., 1872), pp. 224-25, footnote.

Fresh buttermilk—This was Lee's favorite bedtime snack, and he thought it could cure anything (LA, p. 153; Flood, p. 41). At the start of the Petersburg siege, Lee drank tainted buttermilk and became ill for several days (SII, p. 183).

9. Rec, p. 348. A different version has Lee replying: "[W]hy, there were a thousand people on Pennsylvania Avenue in Washington the other day admiring this hat!" (Fitzhugh Lee, *General Lee: A Biography of Robert E. Lee,* reprint, New York: De Capo Press, 1994, p. 408).

Many years after hearing Lee speak about one such Baltimore crowd, Reverend John Leyburn recorded that their chat was about newspapers in the North (Douglas Southall Freeman, *R. E. Lee: A Biography,* vol. 4, New York: Charles Scribner's Sons, 1946, pp. 400-401).

General Lee felt sad that these papers continued to claim that the purpose of the war was to continue slavery. This issue really hurt him, and he denied it. He said he had freed "most of his slaves before the war" started, and those who wanted to go to Liberia, he obliged. They even wrote him tender letters while the war was in progress. There was proof to him that the former slaves did not think he meant them any harm:

> [D]uring this visit to Baltimore some of them who had known him when he was stationed there had come up in the most affectionate manner and put their hands into the carriage window to shake hands with him. They would not have received him in this way, he thought, had they looked upon him as fresh from a war intended for their oppression and injury (ibid.).

According to his son, William Henry Fitzhugh "Rooney" Lee, Robert E. Lee "never owned more than some half-dozen slaves" (FI, p. 371). Lee may have inherited these slaves.

During Lee's only postwar trip to the Deep South, a young teenager wanted to catch a glimpse of the General. The lad wound his way through the masses until he was standing next to Lee, and then gazed respectfully at him. The young man's name was Woodrow Wilson (FIV, pp. 448-49).

10. FI, pp. 132-33. According to author John Perry, Lee's wife Mary ("my Dame") was not in the room when her sister-in-law Nanie prankishly presented Lee to some young ladies as Nanie's younger sibling (LA, p. 101). Douglas Southall Freeman explained: "[Lee] delighted in an occasional prank, and he could play with much satisfaction a mock-serious role" (John L. Gignilliat, "A Historian's Dilemma: A Posthumous Footnote for Freeman's R. E. Lee," *The Journal of Southern History*, 43, May 1977: p. 231).

Andrew Talcott—He was a pen pal and confidant of Lee (Fellman, pp. 24-25, 33, 63). Talcott, Lee's "immediate superior" at Fort Monroe, finished second in his West Point class, as Lee did eleven years later (FI, p. 103).

11. Clifford Dowdey, *Lee* (Boston: Little, Brown, 1965), p. 686.

According to author Margaret Sanborn, when Lee was a cadet at West Point, he liked to be involved in theater performances (Margaret Sanborn, *Robert E. Lee,* vol. 1, Philadelphia: J. B. Lippincott, 1966, p. 61).

12. Douglas Southall Freeman, *R. E. Lee: A Biography*, vol. 2 (New York: Charles Scribner's Sons, 1937), pp. 485-86.

Jeb—James Ewell Brown Stuart was: a cadet at West Point when Lee was the superintendent; a close friend of Lee's daughter Mary; an assistant to Lee in capturing John Brown at Harper's Ferry in 1859; a general in the Confederate cavalry; mortally wounded toward the end of the war (Coulling, pp. 41, 73-74, 98ff., 137). According to author Michael Fellman, Lee and Stuart were cousins (Fellman, pp. 154, 220). Spirits—There was a wine cellar at Arlington; also, the Lees used wine and brandy for medicinal purposes (Coulling, p. 77; Clifford Dowdey and Louis H. Manarin, eds., *The Wartime Papers of R. E. Lee,* Boston: Little, Brown, 1961, pp. 756, 765, 768). When Lee desired to celebrate the surrender of Vera Cruz during the Mexican-American War, he asked his brother to get "a box or two of claret, one of brandy" for the occasion (SI, p. 172).

During the retreat from Petersburg, Lee and others were invited to the home of Judge James H. Cox for a dinner party. The drinks were "Mint juleps." Lee hardly "touched his" before drinking some "ice water" instead. Then the General informed Miss

Kate Cox, "Do you know . . . that this glass of water is, I believe, far more refreshing than the drinks they are enjoying so much?" (FIV, p. 60). After the war, Lee urged young men to use "habitual temperance" concerning hard liquor (Fellman, p. 252).

13. FII, pp. 497-98. On the question of promotions, Lee once replied: 'What do you care about rank? I would serve under a corporal if necessary'" (Marshall W. Fishwick, *Lee after the War,* New York: Dodd, Mead, 1963, p. 95).

One of [Lee's] brigadiers asked him one day, "Why is it, general, that you do not wear the full insignia of your rank, but content yourself with the stars of a colonel?"

"Oh," replied the modest chieftain, "I do not care for display. And the truth is, that the rank of colonel is about as high as I ought ever to have gotten or, perhaps, I might manage a good cavalry brigade if I had the right kind of subordinates" (Rev. J. William Jones, DD, *Personal Reminiscences of Gen. Robert E. Lee,* New York: D. Appleton, 1875, p. 148).

Author Richard McCaslin claims: "Like his idol [George Washington], Lee wore the uniform of a colonel throughout the war" (Richard B. McCaslin, *Lee in the Shadow of Washington,* Baton Rouge: Louisiana State University Press, 2001, p. 78). While Lee lived at Arlington, he could see daily a portrait of George Washington dressed "in the uniform of a militia colonel." When the portrait was competed in 1796, it was "the last to be done of the first president from life" (ibid., p. 28).

While tensions mounted with the possible election of Abraham Lincoln as president, Lee was still in Texas. He may have been jesting when he wrote: "Tell my friends to give me all the promotion they can" (SI, p. 298). Lee was not one to seek promotional favors even though he was still a captain more than two decades after he had graduated from West Point (Fishwick, p. 95). He once wrote: "I know how those things are awarded at Washington, and how the President will be besieged by claimants. . . . I do not wish to be numbered among them" (ibid.).

14. FIV, p. 297. Soon after the battle of Gettysburg, one of the chaplains told Lee that "their most fervent prayers were offered in his behalf." At that point, "tears started in his eyes, as he relied, 'I sincerely thank you for that, and I can only say that I am a poor sinner, trusting in Christ alone for salvation, and that

I need all the prayers you can offer for me'" (L&L, p. 467).

15. FI, p. 113. Also Lee felt that the military could have done more to help him get to the occasion: "[H]as [it] never entered the dull heads of Congress that I ought to be there?" (ibid.).

16. Ibid. "Gilderoy"—He was a "Scottish highwayman" (SI, p. 90). Lee had befriended Eliza MacKay while he was stationed in Georgia (Fellman, pp. 31-32).

17. Ibid., p. 114.

18. SII, pp. 86-87. Lee's "sorrows" were due to the death of his second-oldest daughter Annie who had died recently of fever (ibid., p. 84).

19. Ibid., pp. 115-16. Stoneman—General George Stoneman was the Federal cavalryman given the task of interdicting Lee's communications between Chancellorsville and Richmond (FII, p. 556).

Shortly after this battle, Lee sent notes to the girls he liked best. He told one lass that she could have some of his hair if she would not chuckle at its graying condition. He winced at the way Northern newspapers had changed this Federal-battle lost into a magnificent triumphant, Lee noted: "It will be incomprehensible news to those engaged in the battle" (SII, pp. 115-16).

20. FII, pp. 339-40.

21. Rec, p. 373.

Traveller—He was Lee's favorite horse. Throughout his life, Lee had at least a dozen horses: Bolivar (SI, p. 91), Creole (FI, p. 245), Santa Anna, Grace Darling (Coulling, pp. 26, 28), Grace Darling's Daughter (SII, p. 88), Tom, Jerry (FI, p. 197), Ajax, Brown Roan, Richmond, Traveller (Fishwick, p. 100), and Lucy Long (SII, p. 76).

Though Lee was generally kind to animals, on several occasions he punished Traveller. Once when an artillery shell hit nearby, Lee became stern with his anxious mount; he feared that Traveller's nervousness might have a demoralizing effect on his soldiers (SII, p. 182). After the war, Lee once lost his composure and unexpectedly whipped the recalcitrant horse who preferred to trot rather than to walk (ibid., p. 318).

22. Ibid., p. 327. The Lees, like many well-to-do Virginians, often took vacations at mountain spas.

By 1856, Lee's wife was seeking relief from arthritis that had caused her to be bedridden. The spring waters were said to have worked "wonders" on the body (Coulling, pp. 61, 70). Some bathed in the waters; others, like Lee, drank it for health reasons (Rec, p. 319). When Lee returned from Texas, he found his wife with her hands and feet twisted by an arthritic condition; she was almost an invalid (Coulling, p. 67). One vacation resort was called White Sulphur Springs. According to author Mary Coulling, six of the resorts were within a few dozen miles of Lexington where the Lees resided (ibid., p. 172). As an invalid, Mrs. Lee usually stayed inside her lodge or on the porch unless she was taken to bathe in the mineral waters. The children took walks about the resort while all enjoyed the good food, dances, and other nighttime entertainment (ibid.).

23. SII, p. 103.

24. Ibid., p. 198. John S. Mosby was "a quasi-guerrilla" leader (Fellman, p. 156).

Numbers of "guerilla units" sprang up on their own at the beginning of the war. Yet by April 1862, the Confederate Partisan Ranger Act gave them recognition. Then-Major Mosby tried to rein in his men tightly and also to coordinate his efforts with Jeb Stuart. When Lee heard that Mosby seemed to be more interested in capturing "suttler's [sic] wagons" than in damaging the enemy, he noted: "I have heard of [Mosby's] men, among them officers, being in the rear of the army selling captured goods, suttler's [sic] stores, &c." If this was true, Lee speculated, Mosby must not have known it was going on (ibid., pp. 220-21).

Mosby provided Lee with so many supplies that the General wished he "had a hundred like him" (Donald H. Winkler, *Lincoln and Booth: More Light on the Conspiracy*, Nashville, Tennessee: Cumberland House, Pub., 2003, pp. 152-54).

25. SII, p. 103.

John B. Hood—He led the valiant Texans. He was wounded at both Gettysburg and Chickamauga. Later he fought at Atlanta where he was given command of the Army of Tennessee. He was relieved of that command in December 1864 after he had "fought his army to pieces." After the war, he married, then sold insurance before dying in 1879 from yellow fever (Noah Andre Trudeau, *Gettysburg: A Testing of Courage*, New York: Harper Collins Publishers, 2002, p. 559).

Colonel Robert H. Chilton—He was "Lee's awkward chief of staff" (Gary W. Gallagher, ed., *Fighting for the Confederacy: The Personal Recollections of General Edward Porter Alexander*, Chapel Hill: The University of North Carolina Press, 1989, p. 369).

26. Gallagher, *Fighting*, pp. 156-57.

General Alexander—He was "Longstreet's premier artillerist." He fought until the Appomattox surrender, then constructed railroads, helped to settle one international border dispute, and authored his memoirs before dying in 1910 (Trudeau, p. 557).

General Longstreet—When "Stonewall" Jackson died, James Longstreet ("Old Pete") became Lee's senior lieutenant. He commanded Lee's First Corps, and Lee tagged him as his "old warhorse" (Stephen W. Sears, *Gettysburg*, New York: Houghton Mifflin Co., 2003, pp. 6, 43, 346).

By the time he entered West Point, Lee was advanced enough in math that before long he was taking the academy's fourth-year math classes. Some of the texts at the academy included: a translation by John Farrar of the *Treatise on Plane and Spherical Trigonometry*, and Bezout Legendre's *Geometry*. At the academy, he also studied physics, engineering, chemistry, and mineralogy; in his last year, he requested an assignment to the Engineer Corps, which was the normal selection for those ranked near the top "on the merit roll" (FI, pp. 58, 73, 82). During the 1830s, Lee was assigned to save the river harbor at St. Louis. It was slowly drying as the Mississippi River pressed outward toward its Illinois bank. By 1838, Lee's winning battle against the meandering river was drawing praises from the city's mayor for his brilliance, conscientiousness, and faithfulness to the job. The mayor also extolled Lee for having:

> none of that coddling, and petty, puerile planning and scheming which men of little minds and small intellectual calibre [*sic*] use to make and take care of their frame. The labors of Robert E. Lee can speak for themselves (ibid., pp. 182-83).

Lee enjoyed studying astronomy more than any other subject (Coulling, p. 120).

27. Fishwick, p. 97.

In March 1847, during the Mexican-American War, Lee had a brush with death. After he had finished working with a group of soldiers, he started to return to his lines along with Lieutenant P. G. T. Beauregard. Both of them slowly eased along the small walkway "cut through" a mound of fallen debris. In an instant, another soldier confronted Lee and Beauregard with "Who goes there?" Thinking that he was an American soldier, Lee shot back: "Friends." Yet, by the time this was said, a shot rang out. The American soldier, who thought that Lee and Beauregard were

Mexicans, had fired his pistol at the pair. His shot came so quickly that no one had time to move. The bullet grazed the left side of Lee's uniform and passed under his arm (FI, p. 229).

Pierre Gustave Toutant Beauregard—Like Lee, he graduated from the United States Military Academy at West Point, New York. He was the Confederate general who would fire on Fort Sumter during April 1861; Abraham Lincoln responded to Beauregard's cannons by calling for 75,000 troops to combat the secession stand taken by South Carolina and other Cotton States. Beauregard was also in command at the battle of Manassas in July 1861 (Douglas Southall Freeman, *Lee's Lieutenants: A Study in Command*, vol. 1, New York: Charles Scribner's Sons, 1943, pp. xxxii, 709). On the edge of Mexico City, Lee was slightly wounded but disregarded the wound and continued to fight (FI, p. 283).

Soon after the victory in Mexico, Lee wrote "jovially" to his friend Jack Mackay: "I think a little lead, properly taken, is good for a man. . . . I am truly thankful, however, that I escaped all internal doses, & only recd. some external bruises, contusions & cuts" (McCaslin, p. 50).

During the battle of Second Manassas (Bull Run), Lee, with several others, scouted out ahead to learn the lay of the land. While they were on that short venture, a sniper's bullet scraped Lee's face. He claimed that the enemy "came near killing me just now" (John M. Taylor, *Duty Faithfully Performed: Robert E. Lee and His Critics*, Dulles, Virginia: Brassey's, 1999, pp. 85-86).

During the battle of the Wilderness, Lee was riding at the front of a column when cannon fire erupted. Though Traveller rarely "reared" up in battle, he did so on this occasion. "While his feet pawed the air a shot passed under his belly, grazing Lee's bootheels" (Dowdey, p. 454). Later in the Wilderness, Lee stood on a house porch and began to examine enemy operations across a nearby river. From this hilly position, he could see "puffs of smoke" from the enemy's cannon. As he stood there reconnoitering and drinking some milk, "a stray cannon ball" hit part of the porch next to him (ibid., p. 462).

28. William J. Johnson, *Robert E. Lee: The Christian* (Reprint. Arlington Heights, Illinois: Christian Liberty Press, n.d.), pp. 40-41.

29. L&L, pp. 184-85.

Card—This is a brush, containing many little stiff wires or spikes, used to help prepare wool by scraping. Lee is comparing his beard with these many tiny wires.

Ugly—Lee is exaggerating for effect by using the hyperbole "ugly" to describe his face. In the early 1830s, he was thought to be "the handsomest man in the Army" (SI, p. 93). His brother Smith was also considered to be very handsome (ibid., p. 63).

Walter Herron Taylor, Lee's adjutant general, first met Lee in 1861. Taylor described the fifty-four-year-old Lee as being in "the zenith of his physical beauty . . . [a]dmirably proportioned, of graceful and dignified carriage, with strikingly handsome features, bright and penetrating eyes" (Fellman, pp. 118-19, 279).

Daughter-in-law Charlotte—She was Mrs. W. H. Fitzhugh Lee. Nicknamed "Chass," she lost one child shortly after this letter was written by Lee; a few months later, she also lost a newborn (Coulling, pp. 105, 112-13). The next year, her wounded husband "Rooney" was home recuperating when a 1500-man Union cavalry force launched a brutal raid to capture him. Afterward, "Charlotte broke down completely" and then later died on Christmas eve while Rooney was in a Northern prison (ibid., pp. 125-27, 132).

30. Rec, p. 409. Few "cowards" could have stayed with Lee's aggressive Army of Northern Virginia for long. A large percentage of his men were listed as wounded, killed, or captured. According to author Gary W. Gallagher, Lee's forces sustained "losses approaching 20 percent in his first half-dozen battles compared to fewer than 15 percent for the Federals" (Gary W. Gallagher, ed. *Lee the Soldier,* Lincoln: University of Nebraska Press, 1996, p. 276).

31. FI, p. 132. Author Margaret Sanborn lists the name of Lee's fellow prankster as Jack Macomb, and she states that the two of them even bowed "with great dignity" at the Secretary of the Treasury as they passed the White House (SI, p. 105).

32. SII, p. 90. Lee ate cold sweet potatoes and boiled vegetables and drank buttermilk for the evening meal. Rarely he had mutton (which he liked the best). If meat was handy, he would stop with the first helping and say: "I should enjoy another piece, but I have had my allowance" (SII, p. 90).

33. LA, p. 130. According to Margaret Sanborn, Mary Custis Lee liked to shop frequently in the city. Her frugal husband feared that such trips might get her "bargains in remnants & worsteds" but also might ruin him in the process (SI, p. 143).

Yet, Lee enjoyed good fashion. While a West Point cadet, he acquired a dress coat for his uniform. It was stitched by a tailor at the academy. In the process, the thrifty Lee had figured out the difference in purchasing a new hat and other accoutrements for his attire. He wrote: "We shall be a grand set of fellows with our gold and silver and if I could only catch some of the grandiloquence of my neighbor . . . , I might hope to rise in the world" (FI, p. 118).

Apparently, Lee overindulged "only" when he bought clothing (such as his uniforms) and horses (Dowdey, p. 74).

34. Fishwick, p. 154.

35. Douglas Southall Freeman, *R. E. Lee: A Biography*, vol. 3 (New York: Charles Scribner's Sons, 1937), p. 395.

Lee, unlike his former commander, General Winfield Scott, was unpretentious about rank and also seems to have taken little advantage of its privileges. Lieutenant Colonel Garnet Wolseley (later a field marshal) was impressed by Lee's simple headquarters (SII, pp. 79-80).

General Stern recalled bringing a telegram to General Lee's tent when he was much younger; he entered and without hesitation put his hand on Lee's shoulder. Lee "was very courteous . . . as if it were an everyday occurrence for boys to punch him on his shoulder" (FIII, p. 350, footnote 6).

After the war, Lee went back to visit Petersburg. Many of his fellow Confederate soldiers made the effort to remove his carriage horses and to pull the carriage themselves. Upon seeing this overt display of hero worship, Lee warned: "If you do so, I shall have to get out and help you." When Lee lived in Lexington, visitors at times left their footwear outside the house in the evening; they thought some servant would clean them. However, there was no servant; so General Lee shined their boots instead (Fishwick, pp. 95-96).

36. Fellman, pp. 20-21.

Award-winning writer Douglas Southall Freeman overlooked the humorous angle of Lee's Canadian story. After examining Lee's letter, Freeman wrongly concluded that Lee and his comrade had accidentally killed "a Canadian lighthouse keeper 'in a scuffle' over the use of his tower for running survey lines" (FI, p. 134, footnote 17). Apparently, the only one who lived on that island was William McCormick, and his residence was eight miles from the lighthouse (Fellman, p. 21). Although the lighthouse was at times tended by McCormick, he more often ignored the structure. He died "of natural causes" in 1840. According to author Michael Fellman, Lee "often used such broad humor in his correspondence" (ibid.; for a full explanation of Lee's letter, see Gignilliat, p. 231).

37. Rec, p. 246. Early in his marriage, Lee would pass the evenings

with his wife by reading. Before bedtime, he read a Bible chapter and prayed (LA, p. 98). Yet, it was later "[i]n Baltimore, Lee heard a sermon that at long last gave him 'blessed assurance'" (Taylor, *Duty*, p. 34). In 1861 during his first campaign, Lee had personal devotions every morning and evening (FI, p. 554). Later during the war instead of telling stories at the campfire, Lee retired to his tent to read; one book he read was the Bible (Fellman, p. 116).

38. L&L, pp. 115-16. Little streams or rivulets—These refer to possible "Brooks" children.

39. Fellman, pp. 255-56.

40. Dowdey, p. 75. General Winfield Scott and some of his soldiers attended a Catholic church in Mexico. After candles were given to each officer, Scott, along with his staff, participated in a ceremonial march. The solemn occasion caused Lieutenant Henry Hunt to recall the old High-Church arguments at Fort Hamilton. While Lee was marching in a dignified manner, Hunt placed his hand on Lee, who responded by leaning over and asking quietly what Hunt wanted. Hunt then reminded him of the High-Church/Low-Church controversy at Fort Hamilton and the humorous statement that Lee had made about it at the time. Then Lee did everything he could to refrain from grinning (SI, p. 173).

41. Coulling, p. 159.

42. LA, p. 124. Lee nicknamed: his brother Sydney Smith Lee as "Rose" (ibid., p. 53); younger Washington College students as "yearlings" (Coulling, p. 166); older Washington College students as "leaders of the herd" (ibid.); his niece Mildred as "'Powhattie,' derived from her native county of Powhatan" (SII, p. 334); Union troops as both "British" and "Philistines" (*Wartime*, pp. 55, 869; see McCaslin, p. 83, for Lee's attempt at "levity" in using the word "British"); one family cat as "The Nipper" because of "the manner . . . he slaughtered our enemies the rats and mice" (SII, p. 320).

43. FIV, p. 116. Gordon explained that Lee gave that facetious message about going to the Tennessee line for a reason. It was Lee's way of telling Gordon to go to the Tennessee line if he were able to escape from Grant's vicious chase (Richard Wheeler, *Witness to Appomattox,* New York: Harper & Row Publishers, 1989, pp. 212-13).

General John Gordon—He was: "the diligent commander of the 6th Alabama" (FII, p. 91); distinguished at the Bloody Angle in the Wilderness fight against Grant and thus named "Major General" (FIII, pp. 305-7, 317-19; FIV, p. 47); one of Lee's most "trusted lieutenants," whom Lee consulted in March 1865 about the final course of action for the Army of Northern Virginia (FIV, pp. 7-8, 10); the one who advanced a "stratagem" for attacking Fort Stedman to disrupt Grant's siege of Petersburg (ibid., p. 14); and the leader of a "small and weary corps," along with Longstreet, at the time Lee retreated from Petersburg (ibid., pp. 58ff).

44. LA, p. 161.

The Lees were socially active in Baltimore and acquired new friends through Lee's sister Anne and her in-law family the Marshalls. The most famous of these new friends was "Jerome Napoleon Bonaparte (the son of Napoleon I's brother, Jerome)." Lee soon formed a close relationship with the Bonapartes and wrote them occasionally. Once, when the Bonapartes were away from the city, Lee wrote them that "[a]ll the Belles of the city are said to be engaged, which has caused the belief in others of their sex, that the millenium [*sic*] is at hand" (SI, p. 205). Lee's letters to Jerome Napoleon Bonaparte often mentioned Jenny Lind, Washington Irving, and several ladies from Baltimore (Fishwick, p. 94).

45. FIV, pp. 469-71.

In the spring of 1863, according to author Marshall Fishwick, Lee suffered from "an 'inflammation of the heart-sac.'" After Lee's surrender, he started labeling the same problem as "rheumatism, lumbago or sciatica." After Lee walked for a while, he would ache frequently "along the breastbone"(Fishwick, pp. 161-62).

Near March 1864, Lee had an illness, could not sleep well, and developed a throat infection that possibly led to "pericarditis" (FII, p. 502). Author Douglas Southall Freeman believed that Lee also had symptoms possibly consistent with "angina" (ibid.).

In 1870 Lee consulted a Baltimore doctor, then he wrote his wife: "Dr. Buckler came in to see me this morning, and examined me, stripped, for two hours. He says he finds my lungs working well, the action of the heart a little too much diffused, but nothing to injure. He is inclined to think that my whole difficulty arises from rheumatic excitement, both the first attack in front of Fredericksburg and the second last winter" (Rec, p. 413). According to Fishwick, Lee's doctors may have wrongly diagnosed angina pectoris as rheumatism (Fishwick, p. 217).

46. FII, pp. 486-87.

Stonewall Jackson—Thomas Jonathan "Stonewall" Jackson, the most famous of all commanders during the war, was mortally wounded at the battle of Chancellorsville a few months after this meeting at the Taylors'. He was so devout in his practice of Christianity that he could note that he did not use the mail system on Sunday for fifteen years until he went into the field (J. I. Robertson, Jr., *Stonewall Jackson: The Man, the Soldier, the Legend*, New York: Macmillan Pub., 1997, p. 650). During the battle of Fredericksburg, when some of Jackson's men saw him praying, they followed his example there on the field of battle (ibid., p. 659).

Unknown to Lee, Jackson had planned to launch a 26,000-man counterattack to drive thousands of the enemy into the cold water; this attack commenced late in the day. Yet, Jackson's massive effort was thwarted by the darkness of nightfall. Several hours later, he visited one of his mortally wounded subalterns, General Maxcy Gregg. Jackson urged Gregg to turn his thoughts to God. Then on his way back to camp, Jackson was asked by one of his men what they should do, since they were the ones who had been invaded by the North. The zealous Jackson shouted: "Kill every man!" (ibid., pp. 660-61, 663).

"Those people"—This was one of the many expressions Lee used for Federal troops (Dowdey, p. 465). In his wartime correspondence, Lee often referred to Federal troops as "the enemy" or "enemy" or "enemies" or "Yankee enemies" (*Wartime*, pp. 14, 69, 73, 75, 78-80, 86, 89, 90, 96, 98, 100, 111, 116, 230, 246, 920).

47. L&L, pp. 299-300. Many years earlier, when the 1849 "National Inaugural Ball" was organized, Robert E. Lee was listed as one of the ball's 230 managers. Another manager was listed as the "Hon. A Lincoln, Ill." Douglas Southall Freeman doubts that this committee ever met (FI, pp. 304-5).

Lee's kin—Lee had innumerable Virginia relatives and even knew "his cousins to the third and fourth generation" (Fishwick, p. 102). Lee's Virginia ancestors had not only populated early Virginia, but they had also markedly influenced the state's early governance. Robert E. Lee's father, former three-time governor of the state, once affirmed: "Virginia is my country; her I will obey, however lamentable the fate" (Dowdey, p. 17).

Douglas Southall Freeman lists public offices held by the descendants of Richard Lee, one of Robert E. Lee's American ancestors. Just a few of these were four who worked in American revolutionary conventions, three governors or acting governors, two Declaration of Independence signers, three Continental Congress members, three who were in the United States Congress, and one who was in the cabinet (FI, p. 165).

Author Michael Fellman lists some Virginia families related to Lee. Some of them are the: Bankheads, Beverleys, Bollings, Byrds, Dabneys, Harrisons, Ludwells, Marshalls, Masons, Stuarts, and Taylors (Fellman, p. 3). To boot, Robert E. Lee had many close cousins from the Carter clan. Lee descended from "King Carter" who had twelve children (ibid., p. 24).

48. Rec, p. 9. At times, Lee would play a complex game called "strategy" with his children. As one of them noted about the game, he had "us all shut up in rooms so that we couldn't get out until he let us" (Coulling, p. 29).

49. Coulling, p. 15. On June 5, 1839, while Lee was in Louisville, he wrote to his wife: "If I could only get a squeeze at that little fellow turning up his sweet mouth to 'keeze Baba!'" (L&L, p. 35). Lee also seems to have used baby talk with children other than his own (SII, p. 254).

50. Coulling, p. 175. Lee was upbeat when he attended that vestry meeting on September 28, 1870. However, part of the church, where vestrymen met, was unheated. Lee conversed with friends and told stories about an old churchman. His doctor was also there and recalled that the General appeared to be tired and red in the face in spite of the chilled damp air (Fishwick, p. 203). After the meeting, Lee returned home late. At the supper table he was unable to speak, so the family immediately put him to bed and called the doctors. His condition deteriorated quickly, and he died on October 12, 1870.

51. LA, p. 97. Mary Custis Lee's family had nearly sixty slaves at Arlington when she was born (ibid., p. 41).

American slave labor was so widespread that even Mary Todd Lincoln and Julia Dent Grant were served by slaves. Mary Todd Lincoln—According to author Jean H. Baker, Mary Todd's father (the future father-in-law of Abraham Lincoln) "kept one slave for every white family member of his household" (Jean H. Baker, *Mary Todd Lincoln: A Biography*, New York: W. W. Norton & Company, 1987, p. 62). Julia Dent Grant—Ulysses S. Grant's wife Julia was given at least four slaves by her father; she used slave labor throughout much of her marriage until at least the Emancipation Proclamation (John A. Carpenter, *Ulysses S. Grant*, New York: Twayne Publishers, Inc., 1970, p. 12; also see John Y. Simon, ed., *The Personal Memoirs of Julia Dent Grant*, Carbondale: Southern Illinois University Press, 1975, pp. 80-81, 82-83; note 17 on page 88 claims that since the state of Missouri did not come under the Emancipation Proclamation, "Julia Grant's slaves probably remained her property until the ratification of the Thirteenth Amendment in [December] 1865.")

52. LA, p. 9.

53. FIV, pp. 282-83. Brigadier General W. N. Pendleton—He was formerly Lee's chief of artillery who became the rector of Lexington's Grace Episcopal Church; he encouraged Lee to accept the Washington College presidency (Fishwick, p. 57). A West Point graduate, Pendleton briefly taught declamation at Washington College; he also conducted Lee's burial service (ibid., pp. 57, 70, 142, 221). Pendleton's battle command—"'Lord have mercy on their souls' 'fire!'—became part of the Confederate legend" (ibid., p. 178).

54. Rem, p. 129.

55. SII, p. 275. At Washington College, Lee labeled youth with too much self-confidence as those who would graduate "in one session" (ibid., p. 289).

56. Flood, p. 137.

57. FIII, pp. 237-38. While Lee was at Charleston during the war, he "seasoned the meal" by means of his "good humor and pleasant jests" (SII, p. 33). Meat was often scarce for Confederate troops:

> General Lee shared the privations of his men. His ordinary allowance for the mess table during this period consisted of "a head of cabbage boiled in salt water, and a 'pone' of cornbread." Meat was eaten only twice a week. An amusing anecdote is related by one of his officers. "General Lee having one day invited some gentlemen to dine with him, the . . . servant was ordered to procure a dish of bacon and cabbage. The company arrived, and sat down before a large dish of cabbage, with a small bit of middling in the centre [*sic*] an island in a sea of cabbage. Upon being asked to partake of the unwonted [*sic*] delicacy, each guest politely declined, and the meat was carried away untasted" (Mason, p. 224).

The next day, General Lee asked for the bacon. The servant was embarrassed to reply that the piece of meat had been borrowed and that it had since been returned to its owner (ibid.).

At times, food, itself, was scarce. Lee's son Robert, Jr., who saw his father frequently during the war, stated: "I was [hungry] for three years" (Rec, p. 85). General Lee's daily dose of self-abnegation, coupled with his disdain for pomp, extended to his choice of dinnerware. Implements on his mess table shared by his staff generally consisted of:

> tin plates, tin cups, tin bowls, everything of tin—and consequently indestructible; and to the annoyance and disgust of the subordinates, who sighed for porcelain, could not or would not be lost. . . . [I]t was only in the last year of the war, while the army was around Petersburg, that a set of [borrowed] china was surreptitiously introduced into the baggage of the headquarters of the army . . . [for a short time] (Walter H. Taylor, *Four Years with General Lee*, reprint, Bloomington: Indiana University Press, 1962, pp. 35-36).

One of Lee's adjutants, Walter H. Taylor, stated that Lee was "never so uncomfortable as when comfortable" (ibid., p. 203).

Lee's sense of self-denial continued after the war. Lee still seems to have been "sleeping on his old camp bed" during his first year at Washington College (Flood, p. 134).

Lee's attitude, while among civilians during the war, seems to have been the same as when he was with his troops. One man, who rode the train with Lee in early 1864, noted: "The General is affable, polite and unassuming and shares the discomforts of a crowded railroad coach with ordinary travelers. General Lee is as unostentatious and unassuming in dress as he is in manner." (This quotation was given by Gary Gallagher as recorded on July 3, 1999, during a *Book TV* program later broadcast on television by C-SPAN2).

58. FIII, pp. 418-19.

General George E. Pickett—He was the Confederate general famous for leading an ill-fated charge ("Pickett's Charge") at the battle of Gettysburg. After the war, Pickett left for Canada; when he returned to the United States, he sold insurance until his death in 1875 (Trudeau, p. 562).

General Richard Anderson—He was A. P. Hill's divisional commander who was promoted to corps level; he almost died in poverty in 1879 (ibid., p. 557).

Ambrose Powell ("A. P.") Hill—He worked for five years for the United States Coast Survey and later became a major general in the Confederate Army (LLI, p. xxix). He was killed during the frantic Petersburg retreat a few days before Lee's surrender (Douglas Southall Freeman, *Lee's Lieutenants: A Study in Command*, vol. 3, New York: Charles Scribner's Sons, 1944, p. 679).

59. FI, p. 136.

60. Coulling, pp. 27-28. After Lee moved to Lexington, his son wrote: "My father was much interested in all the arrangements of the house, even to the least thing. He would laugh merrily over the difficulties that appalled the rest of us" (Rec, p. 204).

61. *Wartime*, p. 428.

These symptoms, according to Margaret Sanborn, were indicative of heart problems (SII, pp. 106-7). Yet, Lee was still making merry. When his daughter Agnes could not come to visit him but instead went to see some of her friends, he wrote that Agnes could have helped to cure him by taking his medicine and getting the doctors away from him. He advised her not to bring a lot of people with her since he was "too weak to stand the knocks & bruises they occasion. My pins are remarkably unsteady at this time & the vigour & violent movements of young women might knock them from under me." Though Lee often shunned strangers, he found himself recovering with "refugee families from Fredericksburg" (ibid., p. 107). He added a note of humorous overstatement for Agnes by telling her how overjoyed he was to be around all those people he did not know (ibid., p. 108).

A month after the battle of Gettysburg, Lee warned President Davis that his health was so poor that it had placed limits on his command ability. He did not believe that his physical strength would allow him to oversee properly the work of his army in the field (Dowdey, p. 403). "Longstreet later noted that 'General Lee suffered during the [Gettysburg] campaign from his old trouble, sciatica'" (ibid., p. 403).

Perry—He was one of nearly two hundred slaves owned by Lee's father-in-law, George Washington Parke Custis. As the administrator of the late Mr. Custis's will, Lee emancipated these slaves; he then "hired Perry [as a] personal [servant] . . . for $8.20 per month and hoped" that Perry would put aside some money for a rainy day. Even though the Custis estate seems to have owed Lee money as late as December 1862, he wanted to take the past year's net proceeds (from work done by the remaining Custis slaves), and devote those proceeds "to their future establishment" (*Wartime*, pp. 378-79, 402).

62. Rec, pp. 245-46. Lee's son Robert, Jr., held the rank of captain in the Confederate Army.

After the war Robert E. Lee marched in local parades, including those with Virginia Military Institute cadets. Yet, according to author Marshall Fishwick, he would march out of step to play down the military aspects of the parade (Fishwick, p. 179).

After Abraham Lincoln was assassinated, a military order prohibited the wearing of any Confederate insignia on clothes. For this reason, many former Confederate soldiers had to remove their jacket buttons and CSA belt buckles. In addition, not more than two former Confederates could gather in public at once (Dowdey, pp. 634-35). After the war, when Lee took a trip to Petersburg, there were restrictions against playing the song "Dixie" (ibid., p. 701).

63. SI, p. 121. During this political hubbub, the editor of a local newspaper praised Lee for remaining aloof from politics and for tending to his task of harnessing the Mississippi River (ibid., pp. 121-22).

Thomas Hart Benton—He, noted as a powerful speaker, was a political cohort of Andrew Jackson and was Missouri's perennial senator; while in Congress, Benton successfully "expunged" a resolution denouncing President Jackson. Nicknamed "Old Bullion," Benton wanted to back U.S. currency with gold or silver (*The Encyclopedia Americana Complete in Thirty Volumes,* vol. 3, New York: Americana Corporation, 1951, pp. 528-29; also see *The World Book Encyclopedia,* vol. 2, Chicago: World Book, Inc., 1988, p. 254).

Martin Van Buren—He was the president and also a crony of Andrew Jackson (*The Encyclopedia Americana,* vol. 27, pp. 664-65). Before Lee went to St. Louis, he was invited by Jackson to a reception where Lee met Martin Van Buren, Daniel Webster, and Washington Irving (McCaslin, p. 44). According to author Michael Fellman, Lee was a Federalist (Fellman, p. 79). In 1857, Lee wrote to his brother-in-law Edward Childe that he was glad to see Childe's newspaper article about the United States being one country. Lee claimed that he only knew of "the United States & their Constitution" (ibid., p. 83).

According to author Douglas Southall Freeman, Lee "became a Whig" because he was sympathetic with the politicians that ran the government throughout most of his time in the United States military (FI, p. 117).

Though many of Lee's relatives had been involved in government, he had no love for politics. Later, he expressed his anxiety about the upcoming 1860 election, claiming that political hacks were too selfish to martyr themselves (Fellman, p. 82). Several candidates ran against Lincoln and split the popular vote, thus helping Lincoln to be elected president. Apparently during the war, Lee recorded in his journal that politicians were so "warped by party feeling, by selfishness, or prejudices, that their minds are altogether unbalanced" and that they were "insane" because of political excitement. After the war, Lee spurned suggestions that he run for Virginia's governorship (ibid., pp. 79, 277). At least two Northern newspapers wanted him to run against Grant for the office of president of the United States (FIV, p. 371).

In the presence of the Swiss artist Frank Buchser, Lee unloaded some burdensome thoughts. He usually did not speak so openly to fellow Americans, nor had he said anything against Jefferson Davis's "performance" as president of the Confederacy or specifically against Davis's refusal to give up after Appomattox. Still speaking highly of Davis's character, Lee said to Buchser that President Davis "was of course, one of the extremist politicians." Buchser reported that Lee blamed the war on politicians, whom he believed were responsible for creating it. He also believed that it was a war that could have been prevented easily but that the Republican party was bent on gaining national control and did not "shrink back from anything" (Flood, pp. 200, 220-21).

64. SI, p. 114. Nabob—This can be a very wealthy or important person.

65. SI, pp. 147-48. Lee was apparently referring to Esculapius, the mythological god of healing, and to Polonius, a talkative character in Shakespeare's *Hamlet*.

Strange medicine—In March 1841, Lee wrote to his friend and former coworker Henry Kayser that he had a sickness that went to his head. "Tomorrow I am going to have 20 leeches and the next day God knows what. Some periods of the day the pain is almost intolerable" (Dowdey, p. 99). Only a few years earlier, when Mary Custis Lee became ill after delivering her first daughter, the doctors wanted to use "bleeding and cupping" (Coulling, pp. 8-9). During the war, Lee had his ill horse Richmond bled, but the steed died (Fitzhugh Lee, p. 180).

Lee the nurse—According to Robert, Jr., Lee had several opportunities to act as a nurse.

This tenderness for the sick and helpless was developed in him when he was a mere lad. His mother was an invalid, and he was her constant nurse. In her last illness he mixed every dose of medicine she took, and was with her night and day.

If he left the room, she kept her eyes on the door till he returned. He never left her but for a short time. After her death, the health of their faithful servant,—Nat, became very bad. My father, then just graduated from West Point, took him to the South, had the best medical advice, a comfortable room, and everything that could be done to restore him, and attended to him himself (Rec, p. 326).

According to author Richard B. McCaslin, this "elderly . . . male slave" had a condition that was "tubercular" (McCaslin, p. 35).

Once when his wife was ill and could not tend to the children, Lee stayed up at night holding his daughter to help alleviate her congestion. A little later when his wife came down with the mumps, and his son young Custis began to teethe, Lee was forced to admit that all of this nursing, plus his girl's "little ways," were not so suitable for "a man of my nervous temperament" (Coulling, p. 9).

In November 1845, Lee and his wife took turns staying up several nights to help their son Rooney who had accidentally sliced off several of his fingertips, quickly sewn back on by a doctor. During those watchful nights, the anxious parents tried to prevent Rooney's nighttime tossing and turning from damaging his fragile digits (LA, pp. 142-43).

Later, "in Petersburg, [Lee] called to see a child in whom he felt a special interest, and finding her sick, begged to be shown to her room. When the mother, who was at a neighbor's for a moment, came home, she found him by the bedside of her sick child, ministering to her comfort and cheering her with his words" (Rem, pp. 410-11). At home after the war, Lee nursed his wife, a rheumatic invalid. In May 1867 she described her impaired condition as being so bad that it was a great feat for her to walk across the room without using her crutches. Thus, Mary was often confined in her "rolling chair" (ibid., p. 243).

"Lee always claimed the honor of wheeling his wife into the dining room for meals" (FIV, pp. 323, 412). While the Lees were vacationing at a Virginia spa called Warm Springs, daughter Mildred had a "low, debilitating fever . . . diagnosed as typhoid." Mrs. Lee was not able to take care of Mildred, and so the responsibility went to General Lee and daughter Agnes. While Mildred was suffering from this illness, she became whimsical, claiming that she could only sleep if her father was near to clasp her hand. So Lee dutifully stayed with her each night at their lodging house. Lee spent much of his life caring for his wife, often an invalid, and his children when sick (ibid., p. 372).

66. Rem, p. 291.

67. Ibid., pp. 290-91.

Fifteen years later, Lee would achieve far-flung fame by driving Union general George B. McClellan's army away from the gates of Richmond. Yet, shortly before he accomplished this feat, worried Richmond citizens were ridiculing Lee as the "King of Spades." They resisted his laborious attempts to fortify the city with many miles of defensive entrenchments. Lee, on the other hand, bemoaned to President Davis that just about everyone in the South was against military labor. Yet, it was the very tool that McClellan was using to advance on Richmond. Lee thought that such labor was important for military goals and for saving lives. He affirmed: "There is nothing so military as labour, and nothing so important to an army as to save the lives of its soldiers." After Lee drove the Federals away from Richmond, this success not only changed the war's early course, it also revived the sagging Southern morale. Later that year after the battle of Fredericksburg, Lee had so fortified one nearby area as to elicit the praise that it was one of the strongest military positions in the world. Author Douglas Southall Freeman noted that such works, put up by Lee near Fredericksburg, represented Lee's "most historic contributions to the science of war" (FII., pp. 86, 480-81).

68. SII, p. 37. When Lee went south to strengthen Confederate coastal defenses, certain South Carolinians distrusted him because of his initial stand against secession. One claimed that Lee's "heart" was against the Confederacy; another suggested that Lee was a "traitor" for even considering the "possibility of retreat." Still Lee continued his task. At one time he responded to a complaint about "the poor quality of" weapons, by saying, "Sir, your people had better write to Mr. Lincoln and ask him to postpone this thing for a few months until you can get ready for him" (SII, pp. 6-7).

Lee on secession—The Lee family was slow to board the secession bandwagon. Lee saw no reason to secede. On the day he sent in his resignation from the United States military, he explained to his sister in Baltimore:

> Now we are in a state of war which will yield to nothing. The whole south is in a state of revolution, into which Virginia,

after a long struggle, has been drawn; and, though I recognize no necessity for this state of things, and would have forborne and pleaded to the end for a redress of grievances, real or supposed, yet in my own person I had to meet the question whether I should take part against my native state (FI, p. 443).

During that same weekend, one of the Lee cousins was visiting at Arlington and bore witness to the family's shock at Virginia's initial decision to secede. Rooney and his brother Custis, inside the mansion house, were dismayed at hearing about secession; yet, those outside in the nearby streets of Alexandria were ecstatic. Custis had graduated first in his class at West Point and was serving in the army; like his father, he thought a revolution was taking place; Rooney was depressed over the elated and jubilant crowds he saw at the Alexandria depot. "The people [he said] . . . had lost their senses and had no conception of what a terrible mistake they were making." Though there was joy all around the town, the atmosphere at Arlington was like a funeral parlor (Coulling, pp. 82-83).

Lee the protector—Even before Virginia's convention voted to secede, in April 1861, Lee was determined to place himself in whatever position needed to help protect his massive Lee/Carter clan. During February, while he was in still in Texas, Lee wrote to his wife's cousin Markie Williams: "I am very desirous to be near those who claim my protection, and who may need my assistance" (Dowdey, p. 125). Ironically, Markie stayed in the North during most of the war.

By the end of the war, Lee would be promoted to "general in command of all Confederate forces" (Flood, p. 3). Each of his sons would fight for the Confederacy—Major General Custis "Boo" Lee, Major General W. H. Fitzhugh "Rooney" Lee, and Captain Robert E. Lee, Jr.

Lee had the prewar belief that the authors of the U. S. Constitution would not have expended so much labor "if [the Constitution] was intended to be broken by every member of the Confederacy at will." He then believed that the Constitution represented a perpetual union. Douglas Southall Freeman admitted that Lee's position had changed during the war: "Lee absorbed the Southern constitutional argument and was convinced by it" (Thomas L. Connelly, *The Marble Man: Robert E. Lee and His Image in American Society,* New York: Knopf, 1977, pp. 34, 56).

69. SII, pp. 94-95.

70. Ibid., p. 118. About this time, Lee, dressed casually and escorted by a detail, looked as though he had been arrested. When

Lee's entourage passed, one soldier from the Seventeenth Mississippi loudly cried: "Boys, where did you get that bushwhacker?" The soldier who called Lee a "bushwhacker" was Sergeant C. C. Cummings. Years later, he recalled how Lee's face brightened upon hearing this laughable pronouncement. "His bright smile . . . haunts me still," Cummings remembered, as late as 1915 (Trudeau, p. 28).

Lee's army had trounced Pope's at the battle of Second Manassas. Before the war, Lee, together with Jeb Stuart and a contingent of Marines, put down John Brown's insurrection at Harper's Ferry, (West) Virginia. Later, during the War Between the States, Stuart was mortally wounded at the battle of Yellow Tavern (Coulling, pp. 73-74, 100-101, 137). After the war, Lee referred to General Stuart as his "ideal of a soldier" (Dowdey, p. 697).

Fitzhugh Lee described Stuart as wearing "a conspicuous [hat], having a broad brim looped up on one side, over which always floated large black feathers. . . . [He] . . . was not adverse to the pomp of war . . . [and] was in all glory with his 'fighting jacket' and dancing plume" (Fitzhugh Lee, pp. 183, 318).

71. Dowdey, pp. 362-63.

After the war, Lee spoke to a minister's daughter who was visiting. "Miss Josie . . . has your father a good hat? . . . I have two good hats, and I don't think a good rebel ought to have two good articles of one kind in these hard times." So he offered her his dress parade hat for her father. Author Douglas Southall Freeman believed that this dress parade hat was probably the hat he had at his surrender (FIV, pp. 209-10). After the war when he returned from a trip where many friends had flocked to see him, Lee reported that "they would make too much fuss over the old rebel" (Rec, p. 348; also see Lee's similar use of the phrase "old Confederate"—ibid., p. 388).

Soon after the war, Lee was asked by a reporter about the subject of treason. He thought back over the beginning of the war and expressed the Southern view that secession was not against the U. S. Constitution. He also allowed that those who participated in secession were not treasonous in their actions. In reference to the Constitutional Convention of 1787, he said that the issue of secession had been discussed at this convention; however, it had remained unsettled. So any war that started because of it could not be thought of as treason. He also claimed that the war would finally settle this issue (Flood, pp. 49-50).

Robert E. Lee national remembrances—Since the early 1900s, Fort Lee, in Virginia, has been the home for the U. S. Army and more recently headquarters for the Quartermaster Corps. For about twenty years, the navy's ballistic submarine, the U.S.S. *Robert E. Lee,* protected the nation's shores. Today, multitudes annually visit the Federal government's Robert E. Lee Memorial mansion on top of a large, verdant hill at Arlington National Cemetery (LA, p. 345).

72. SII, p. 192. When Lee wrote to his wounded nephew, he claimed that Fitz had grown a long beard in "hopes . . . [that] like the shield of Achilles," it would "turn aside the darts of such fair archers. Cupid is always busy when Mars is quiet & our young heroes think it necessary to be killed in some way"(ibid., pp. 192-93).

73. Rem, pp. 243-44.

74. SII, pp. 258-59.

75. Ibid., p. 334. One of Lee's idols was George Washington who told jokes during tea time at Mount Vernon (Henry Wiencek, *An Imperfect God: George Washington, His Slaves, and the Creation of America,* New York: Farrar, Straus and Giroux, 2003, p. 345). Lee's father had an unexpected "sense of humor" and a talent for making new phrases, which was something his children did not forget (Gerson, p. 4; Dowdey, pp. 9, 25).

76. Rec, p. 380. Lee's daughter Mildred was enthusiastic in ways that pleased her father; he even called her the "light bearer," thus proclaiming that "the house is never dark when she is in it!" Still, he continued to pick on this pet daughter about the clarity of her handwriting, how much she weighed, and about her propensity to dispense advice that no one requested (Coulling, p. 170). Lee often teased his daughters about their household arts (Rec, p. 205). During the war, he playfully wrote to one of his daughters on her sixteenth birthday: "You know it is considered vulgar for young ladies to eat, which I suppose is the cause of your abstinence. But do not carry it too far" (L&L, pp. 159-60).

77. SII, pp. 363-64.

78. Philip Van Doren Stern, *Robert E. Lee, the Man and the Soldier: A Pictorial Biography* (New York: Bonanza Books, 1963), p. 238.

Before Lee attended West Point, he would draw cone diagrams on a slate board. Even though he was aware that each drawing would be erased before another was drawn, his drawings were precise and accurate just as though they were engravings or printings (FI, pp. 46-47).

After taking drawing classes at West Point, he was first stationed in Georgia; there he sketched in detail a terrapin, an alligator, and Napoleon reclining in death (SI, pp. 178ff.). In the 1850s, when

Lee was the superintendent of West Point, he called one of his cadets "little Jimmy Whistler" (ibid., p. 297). Lee made the following observation about him: "I wish indeed that he may succeed in his career. He certainly has talent, if he could acquire application." Jimmy was unable to graduate from West Point (ibid., pp. 297-98 and pp. 224-35). "Little Jimmy," James McNeill Whistler, became famous for his portrait known as *Whistler's Mother* (*The World Book Encyclopedia*, vol. 21, p. 285).

79. Flood, pp. 134-35.

80. Rem, p. 411.

81. Ibid., p. 288.

82. Ibid., p. 242.

83. Dowdey, p. 549.

84. Stanley F. Horn, ed. *The Robert E. Lee Reader* (New York: The Bobbs-Merrill Co., 1949), pp. 485-86.

85. Ibid., pp. 486-87.

Fitzhugh Lee—He was a major general in the Confederate cavalry. After the war, he became: the governor of Virginia; an American consul-general to Cuba; a major general in the United States volunteers (with the Seventh Army Corps); the military governor of Havana; and the commander of the Department of Missouri (*The Encyclopedia Americana*, vol. 17, p. 182).

86. SII, p. 287.

87. Coulling, p. 69. When Lee wrote this letter, Custis was on a military assignment taking him to California. Custis's grandfather had willed to him Arlington plantation (LA, pp. 341-42 and pp. 33-34.). According to author Clifford Dowdey: "The fact was that the Lee men were very good marriers as a rule and frequently improved their estates through wives" (Dowdey, p. 7).

Lee and his father married into two of Virginia's wealthiest families. Lee's father was a widower who sought comfort in a prospective bride named Ann Hill Carter. He met Ann while he was visiting Shirley plantation on the James River; the plantation belonged to Charles Carter, a Virginian, whose wealth was scarcely surpassed by anyone in the state, except George Washington (FI, p. 8). Lee's widowed father married Ann Hill Carter, who gave birth to Robert E. Lee in 1807. Robert E. Lee married George Washington's step-great-granddaughter, Mary Anna Randolph Custis (LA, pp. 13, 81, 347, and Rec, p. 337).

88. Coulling, p. 166.

Gossip—Lee was not innocent of "harmless gossip" in his letters

(SI, p. 140). He also enjoyed gossiping with his daughters (Fellman, p. 242). A reader—As a youngster, Lee read in school "all the minor classics in addition to Homer & Longinus, Tacitus & Cicero" (FI, p. 40). He also "reread . . . Homer, Caesar, Hafiz the Persian, Shakespeare, and Cervantes" (SI, p. 40). On the day Mary Custis agreed to marry him, he had been reading to her from a new Sir Walter Scott novel (FI, p. 104). Even though he could quote "line after line" from Scott's *Lady of the Lake,* he advised his daughter Mildred : "Read history, works of truth, not novels and romances" (Rec, p. 10; also see Fishwick, p. 134). Lee seems to have taken out fewer than fifty books from Lexington libraries (Fishwick, p. 135). The year 1867 seems to have signaled a distinct change in his preference for reading; at that time, Lee no longer selected library books about American history or about biography (ibid.). He became president of the Rockbridge County Bible Society and regularly read the Bible; he claimed that the Bible "never failed to give" him "light and strength" (L&L, p. 470).

89. FIII, pp. 235-36.

90. SII, p. 165.

91. Ibid.

92. FI, pp. 364-65.

93. Ibid., p. 118.

94. Fishwick, p. 103.

95. SII, p. 88.

96. Rem, p. 413. According to Marshall Fishwick, like other Tidewater relatives, as Lee grew older he viewed kisses from young ladies as his right. One of his kin, Thomas H. Carter, regularly rendezvoused with the horse-drawn coaches; after asking each lass who was disembarking, "What might your name be, dear: I think you're a kinswoman of mine." Tom Carter then proceeded to bestow a welcome kiss (Fishwick, p. 101).

97. SI, pp. 52-53. According to one of Lee's cousins, after young Robert recovered from the grief of his mother's death, he was "as full of life, fun and particularly of teasing, as any of us" (FI, p. 92).

98. SI, p. 38. Not everyone was as relaxed with George Washington as was Henry Lee, Robert E. Lee's father. "Friends and foes alike noticed that [Henry] was one of the few who could banter with the stiff Washington" (McCaslin, p. 16).

One time Washington went into a room filled with acquaintances of one of his stepchildren. When that happened, everyone suddenly quit talking. His stepchild remembered a certain "awe and respect he inspired. . . . [H]is own near relatives feared to speak or laugh before him" (Wiencek, pp. 6-7).

On election day, when Henry "Light-Horse Harry" Lee was running for national congress, a towering, slender man, dressed in costly garments, arrived at the poll to cast his vote. He got off his horse and slightly bowed his head; those around him eagerly waited to learn the candidate of his choice. Though voters were usually required to prove ownership of one hundred acres before they could vote, such proof was not necessary in this case. Soon, the head of the election board asked this slender voter: "Your vote, sir?" The prospective voter responded loudly: "I cast my vote for Major General Henry Lee of Stratford." He then tipped his hat, mounted his horse, and left for home. That towering gentleman was George Washington. Major General Henry "Light-Horse Harry" Lee won this election by a narrow margin (Gerson, pp. 209-10). When Washington died, Henry Lee wrote the famous description of the first president: "First in war, first in peace, first in the hearts of his countrymen" (Johnson, p. 23).

99. SI, p. 92.

Richard "Dick" Tilghman—He was a West Point graduate and a groomsman at Lee's wedding (LA, p. 82). Also, he was one of Lee's "old set" of bachelor friends at Fort Monroe (SI, p. 91).

100. Rec, p. 316. During the last year of the war, not every gift Lee received was edible. One unknown donor sent a pair of spurs; a judge sent a saber. Gloves, a new hat, and a well-carved pipe also arrived. Yet when Lee was not sure what to do with the pipe, he asked his son Robert for advice. When no advice came from Robert, Jr., Lee sent the pipe to Richmond for "safekeeping" and wrote: "I infer that [Robert] does not recommend my indoctrination into the [odorous] art, as he has withheld his desired advice. I fear it is rather late for me to learn anything good" (SII, p. 162). Lee claimed that chewing tobacco was obnoxious to him (Flood, pp. 106-7).

101. Coulling, p. 161, footnote.

102. LA, p. 272.

103. Ibid. Lee, an accomplished military engineer, once embarrassed himself with his own record keeping. In 1845 when he was overseeing monotonous work in New York, there was an error made that led to Lee's being paid two times during May and June. He lamented that this error "has caused me more mortification . . . than any other act of my life, to find that I have

been culpably negligent where the strictest accuracy is both necessary and required" (FI, p. 200).

During the war, Lee's soldiers were often pitifully supplied. In
the daytime his daughters knit socks for the troops; at night they
read a French novel, *Les Miserables,* new to Richmond. The Lee
girls and others tenderly changed the title to "Lee's Miserables,"
befitting his troops who were lightly clad and exposed to the freezing weather at their winter camp (Coulling, p. 132).

104. Rec, pp. 200-201.

105. LA, pp. 153-54. At the battle of Second Manassas (Second
Bull Run), Lee was looking through his binoculars when Captain
Mason of his staff told him that someone needed to see the
General. Lee then noticed a powder-covered gunner nearby. Yet,
the General was not startled; he was used to being stopped by even
the most common volunteer soldier wanting to speak to him for
almost any reason. Because of this familiarity with the troops, Lee
asked: "Well, my man, what can I do for you?" "Why, General," the
young man responded with a troubled but recognizable voice,
"don't you know me?" The young man was his own son, Robert, Jr.
(FII, pp. 335-36).

106. LA, p. 164. One of Lee's professors, J. J. White, had a very
close relationship with Lee. The two went on long rides from time
to time. On one occasion the two had to stay all night at a farm
where there was only one bed. When Professor White contemplat-
ed sleeping in the same bed with Lee, he recalled: "I would as soon
have thought of sleeping with the Archangel Gabriel as with the
General!" His commentary on the situation: "No man was great
enough to be intimate with General Lee" (Fishwick, pp. 180-81;
compare with SII, p. 292). At family functions, it was not unexpected for three kinfolk to sleep in one bed (FI, p. 133).

107. SI, pp. 308-9. According to author Marshall Fishwick, Lee
was not a scholar. "His own sentences reveal occasional errors in
grammar and syntax" (Fishwick, p. 134).

108. LA, pp. 91-92.

109. SI, p. 92.

110. Ibid., p. 206.

111. Flood, p. 140. According to author Charles B. Flood, Mary
was aware of her husband's "need to look upon the youthful beauty she could not provide." She also knew how greatly he enjoyed
his lighthearted talk in connection with the manners he had

learned in the South. Shortly after he died, she claimed: "No one enjoyed the society of women more than himself. It seemed the greatest recreation in his toilsome life" (ibid., p. 140).

112. Fellman, p. 134. The Lees, like many other families, had relatives who fought on opposing sides during the war. Lee's sister, Anne Marshall, lived in Baltimore; her son Louis had attended West Point and fought with Union general John Pope (Coulling, pp. 28, 106).

113. SII, p. 110. In other situations, Lee seemed more reserved with his laughter. Although he had a "good sense of humor," his bearing seldom allowed him to laugh in public. Yet to some of those near him, he seemed to "laugh inwardly" (FI, p. 451).

114. Coulling, p. 42.

115. Ibid., p. 64. After the war, Lee put on his Confederate uniform only a few times (Fishwick, p. 180). He believed that his greatest mistake had been to take a military education because it stifled character development (Fellman, p. 250). After the war and decades of military service, Lee had finally grown accustomed to civilian life, and so he wrote to General Richard Stoddert Ewell in 1868: "I much enjoy the charms of civil life . . . and find too late that I have wasted the best years of my existence" (FIV, p. 363). When sixty-two years old, Lee finally affirmed: "I am a soldier no longer" (Flood, p. 219).

116. Fitzhugh Lee, pp. 232-33. Concerning pet chickens, Lee wrote to his daughter Mildred after the war, "I suppose Robert [Jr.] would not eat [your chickens] 'Laura Chilton' and 'Don Ella McKay.' Still less would he devour his sister 'Mildred'" (Rec, p. 193).

117. LA, p. 131. While at Fort Hamilton, Mary Custus Lee was particularly interested in the welfare of four former Arlington slaves, then freed and living in New York (ibid., p. 138).

Mary focused her concern on one named Cassy whose mother had been the governess of Mary's father; and, after all these years, Cassy's mother still served at Arlington. Mary was able to locate Cassy by means of Lily, who had also been a servant. Lily's husband, Eddison, had a job in the area as a steamboat steward. Though Lily and Eddison were having no trouble in New York, Cassy and her husband, Louis, were struggling. Just before the new year, Louis's sickness forced them to sell everything but their clothes to pay for his medical bills and the rent. And Cassy started washing clothes to help pay for their food and lodging. So, Mary

Lee's mother invited Cassy to come back to the Arlington area in hopes that she could find better pay for a while. Cassy did come to spend the night with Mary at Fort Hamilton, but she did not accept the offer to return South. She could not leave her husband, and also she was "too embarrassed" to go back home in a destitute condition. Mary offered to help the struggling couple with boat passage to the Arlington area; she also gave Cassy "some money & some things" to carry back with her (ibid., p. 138).

118. Fishwick, p. 151. Mildred's advice to "young mothers" is ironic since neither she nor any of her sisters married. The year before he died, Lee wrote: "We are all as usual—the women of the family very fierce, and the men very mild" (Fellman, p. 293).

One of the most headstrong of Lee's daughters was his oldest, Mary. Most of the people in the South had no idea what to expect from her. They appreciated her courage and venturesome manner, yet were forced to view her in a different light from her father. Why? Once Mary was arrested! During 1902, in Alexandria, Virginia, Mary was arrested for apparently breaking a Jim Crow law. She had stepped aboard a streetcar with her maid, then proceeded to sit down with the maid in the back of the conveyance, the rear portion of which was reserved for minority passengers. When a request was made for Mary to move up front, she refused and then was arrested. She posted a small bond but did not appear in court when asked to do so. Mary's stubborn actions seem to have been spawned by her own personal objections to this Jim Crow law which interfered with the normal way she traveled with her maid (Coulling, pp. 189-90).

119. Coulling, p. 164. The Lee girls could not have been considered prudish by Lexington standards (ibid., pp. 164-65).

They not only had gentlemen callers, they also took lengthy walks and rode on horses and in sleighs. Mary and Agnes, to the chagrin of some locals, went on one sleigh ride with two VMI bachelor faculty members; the four, unsupervised, did not return until about dark. The Lee girls also ice skated, which only "Yankee women" were thought to have done before the Lees came to Lexington. The girls attended debates and lectures and went to dances. One VMI dance lasted until three o'clock in the morning. They even attended a circus, though "before the war, a circus had not been considered a very high class entertainment." Even General Lee accompanied them! His presence caused one of Agnes's friends to remark that General Lee's appearance, as president of

Washington College, "lent dignity even to a circus" (ibid., 165-66).

120. Coulling, pp. 170-71.

121. Fellman, p. 29.

122. SI, p. 73.

123. Fellman, p. 136.

124. J. Steven Wilkins, *Call of Duty: The Sterling Nobility of Robert E. Lee* (Nashville, Tennessee: Cumberland House Pub., 1997), pp. 263-64.

125. Coulling, p. 130.

126. Wilkins, p. 264.

127. Coulling, p. 83.

128. Rec, pp. 194-95.

Bremo—This was a 1500-acre estate west of Richmond belonging to Dr. Cocke and his family (ibid., p. 139). Sally Warwick—Sally, from Richmond, was an acquaintance of Agnes Lee; she was also an "inveterate flirt" engaged to Lee's "confirmed bachelor" son Custis (Coulling, p. 130).

Agnes—She was Lee's third-oldest daughter who only lived to be thirty-two years of age; she died, three years to the week, after her father did. Lee's widow Mary was so despondent at Agnes's sudden and unexpected death, that Mary only lived three weeks after her daughter's demise (ibid., pp. 179-80).

129. Rec, pp. 261-62.

130. Ibid., pp. 307-9.

Lee was always eager for his sons to marry; on the other hand, he enjoyed having his daughters at home. None of them married. "Daughter" Mary became a world traveler after Lee died, and she lived outside of the United States for a time. Lee's son Robert, Jr., first married Charlotte Haxell, who died within a year; next he married Juliet Carter. Robert, Jr., inherited the Romancoke estate from his grandfather Custis. Lee's son Fitzhugh's first wife, Charlotte Wickham, died during the war; Fitzhugh next married Mary Tabb Bolling. From his grandfather Custis, Fitzhugh inherited the White House estate where George and Martha Washington wed (Coulling, pp. 169, 167-68, 177-78, 184, 198ff.).

After he was married, Lee wrote Fitzhugh to advise him "not to depend entirely on sentiment" but to make thorough arrangements for his bride's material needs. In urging this action, the sixty-one-year-old Lee seemed to quote, in part, from the old English nursery rhyme "The Little Man and the Little Maid." Lee wrote: "It is good that the wheat is doing so well, for I am not sure 'that the flame you are so rich in will light a fire in the kitchen, nor the little god turn the spit, spit, spit'" (Rec., pp. 309-10). In that poem, the little man wants to marry the little maid, but she naturally asks him how they will eat. Then she repeats the line that Lee quoted. To which the little man replies, "My offers are but small, but you have my little all and what we have not got we must borrow, borrow, borrow." Lee may have been subtly and lightheartedly warning Fitzhugh neither to go into debt nor to borrow money from outsiders. Lee feared debt; it had caused his father to spend time in jail in the early 1800s.

131. SI, p. 100. Rip Raps—This was the nickname for old Fort Calhoun near Fort Monroe where Lee was stationed (ibid., p. 96).

At Fort Monroe, Lee and his wife first shared quarters that consisted of "two dirt-floored rooms." Such ground-floor accommodations required an enormous adjustment for Mary Custis Lee who had grown up in the spacious Arlington mansion (LA, p. 86). The Lees later moved upstairs at Fort Monroe to "preferred quarters" on the second floor (Dowdey, p. 56). Part of Lee's irritation, as expressed in this letter, concerned an ongoing feud, between engineers (like Lee) and other officers, about the use of "living quarters within the fort" (SI, p. 100).

Punctilio—This can be the observance of small details.

132. Coulling, p. 121. Mildred did not need many new clothes because most of her friends dressed very simply during the war. "Hoop skirts, if worn at all, were smaller than antebellum petticoats, and dresses were often remade from old silks and cambrics." Because the Union Navy blockaded Confederate harbors, shortages included hairpins and hair nets (ibid.).

133. SI, p. 296. Salamander—This could be many different things or creatures associated with heat or fire.

A swimmer—Lee had been an excellent swimmer since childhood. His son, Robert, Jr., recalled: "My father always encouraged me in every healthy outdoor exercise and sport . . . [w]ith swimming, . . . he was very anxious I should learn in a proper manner." After Robert, Jr., took some swimming lessons, he said that his father "inquired constantly how I was getting along, explaining to me what he considered the best way to swim, and the reasons [therefore]" (Rec, pp. 13-14).

134. SII, pp. 206-7.

135. FIV, pp. 411-12.

136. FIII, pp. 233-34.

137. This incident is taken from author James Perry's statement recorded November 8, 2003, during a *Book TV* program broadcast by C-SPAN2. Perry is the author of *Touched with Fire: Five Presidents and the Civil War Battles That Made Them*. Lee's facetiousness in mentioning "pikes" may have an interesting background. According to author Thomas Flagel, during 1862 Stonewall Jackson made a request for companies to receive pikes; General Lee agreed with the request. The governor of Georgia ordered thousands of pikes for the state militia; he even declared that the weapons could be put to good use against the enemy's cavalry (Thomas R. Flagel, *The History Buff's Guide to the Civil War*, Nashville, Tennessee: Cumberland House, 2003, p. 107).

138. McCaslin, p. 155.

139. Fitzhugh Lee, p. 76. Early in the war, General Lee was fighting in West Virginia with one of the last Washington descendants to live at Mount Vernon. When this young man, who was very close to the General, was killed, Lee wrote to his daughter about the death. To help alleviate this loss, he joyously included a note about the family cat at Arlington (at that time under Union control). Since his daughter Mildred was concerned about the cat's safety, Lee promised that "he would 'get Genl Johnston to send in a flag of truce and make inquiries'" about getting the cat back! Johnston was a high-ranking Confederate general at that time (McCaslin, p. 94).

140. SII, p. 233. Just after Lee's surrender at Appomattox, Union general Meade visited. Though still under the great "burden" of defeat, Lee was able to show good cheer in the presence of his guest. As the two met, Lee "asked jovially" why General Meade's "beard had gotten so gray." Meade responded "that Lee was responsible for most of it" (McCaslin, p. 192). Lee first fought against Meade at the battle of Gettysburg.

141. L&L, p. 241.

142. Rec, p. 21.

143. Ibid., p. 12.

Selected Bibliography

Baker, Jean H. *Mary Todd Lincoln: A Biography*. New York: W. W. Norton & Company, 1987.

Carpenter, John A. *Ulysses S. Grant*. New York: Twayne Publishers, Inc., 1970.

Connelly, Thomas L. *The Marble Man: Robert E. Lee and His Image in American Society*. New York: Knopf, 1977.

Coulling, Mary P. *The Lee Girls*. Winston-Salem, N.C.: John F. Blair Pub., 1987.

Dowdey, Clifford. *Lee*. Boston: Little, Brown, 1965.

Dowdey, Clifford, and Louis H. Manarin, eds. *The Wartime Papers of R. E. Lee*. Boston: Little, Brown, 1961.

Fellman, Michael. *The Making of Robert E. Lee*. New York: Random House, 2000.

Fishwick, Marshall. W. *Lee after the War*. New York: Dodd, Mead, 1963.

Flagel, Thomas R. *The History Buff's Guide to the Civil War*. Nashville, Tenn.: Cumberland House, 2003.

Flood, Charles Bracelen. *Lee: The Last Years*. Boston: Houghton Mifflin, 1981.

Freeman, Douglas Southall. *Lee's Lieutenants: A Study in Command*, vol. 1. New York: Charles Scribner's Sons, 1943.

Freeman, Douglas Southall. *Lee's Lieutenants: A Study in Command*, vol. 3. New York: Charles Scribner's Sons, 1944.

Freeman, Douglas Southall. *R. E. Lee: A Biography*, 4 vols. New York: Charles Scribner's, Sons, 1937-1946.

Gallagher, Gary W., ed. *Fighting for the Confederacy: The Personal Recollections of General Edward Porter Alexander*. Chapel Hill: The University of North Carolina Press, 1989.

——. ed. *Lee the Soldier*. Lincoln: University of Nebraska Press, 1996.

Gerson, Noel B. *Light-Horse Harry, A Biography of Washington's Great Cavalryman, General Henry Lee*. Garden City, N.Y.: Doubleday, 1966.

Gignilliat, John L. "A Historian's Dilemma: A Posthumous Footnote for Freeman's R. E. Lee," *The Journal of Southern History*, 43 (May 1977).

Horn, Stanley F., ed. *The Robert E. Lee Reader*. New York: The Bobbs-Merrill Co., 1949.

Johnson, William J. *Robert E. Lee: The Christian.* Reprint. Arlington Heights, Illinois: Christian Liberty Press, n.d.

Jones, Rev. J. William, DD. *Life and Letters of Robert Edward Lee, Soldier and Man.* Reprint. Harrisonburg, Va.: Sprinkle Publications, 1986.

———. *Personal Reminiscences of Gen. Robert E. Lee.* New York: D. Appleton, 1875.

Lattimore, Ralston B., ed. *The Story of Robert E. Lee as told in his own words and those of his contemporaries.* Source Book Series, No. 1, Philadelphia: Eastern National Park & Monument Assoc., 1964.

Lee, Fitzhugh. *General Lee: A Biography of Robert E. Lee.* Reprint. New York: De Capo Press, 1994.

Lee, Capt. Robert E. *Recollections and Letters of General Robert E. Lee.* Reprint. New York: Garden City Pub., 1924.

Mason, Emily V. *Popular Life of Gen. Robert Edward Lee.* Baltimore: John Murphy & Co., 1872.

McCaslin, Richard B. *Lee in the Shadow of Washington.* Baton Rouge: Louisiana State University Press, 2001.

Perry, John. *Lady of Arlington: The Life of Mrs. Robert E. Lee.* Sisters, Oregon: Multnomah Pub., 2001.

Robertson, James I., Jr. *Stonewall Jackson: The Man, the Soldier, the Legend.* New York: Macmillan Pub., 1997.

Sanborn, Margaret. *Robert E. Lee,* 2 vols. Philadelphia: J. B. Lippincott, 1966-67.

Sears, Stephen W. *Gettysburg.* New York: Houghton Mifflin, 2003.

Simon, John Y., ed. *The Personal Memoirs of Julia Dent Grant.* Carbondale: Southern Illinois University Press, 1975.

Stern, Philip Van Doren. *Robert E. Lee, the Man and the Soldier: A Pictorial Biography.* New York: Bonanza Books, 1963.

Taylor, John M. *Duty Faithfully Performed: Robert E. Lee and His Critics.* Dulles, Va.: Brassey's, 1999.

Taylor, Walter H. *Four Years with General Lee.* Reprint. Bloomington: Indiana University Press, 1962.

Trudeau, Noah Andre. *Gettysburg: A Testing of Courage.* New York: Harper Collins Pub., 2002.

Wiencek, Henry. *An Imperfect God: George Washington, His Slaves, and the Creation of America.* New York: Farrar, Straus and Giroux, 2003.

Wilkins, J. Steven. *Call of Duty: The Sterling Nobility of Robert E. Lee.* Nashville, Tenn.: Cumberland House Pub., 1997.

Winkler, H. Donald. *Lincoln and Booth: More Light on the Conspiracy.* Nashville, Tenn.: Cumberland House Pub., 2003.

Index

afghan, 20
Alexander (the Great), 17
Alexander, Gen. Porter, 25
Alexandria, 26, 62
Amelia Court House, 46
ammunition, 24
animals, 28, 45, 47, 49-50, 57-58
apple tree, 67
Appomattox, 27, 46, 67
arithmetic, 53
Arlington (Virginia), 17
Arlington (Lee mansion), 36, 47, 58
Army of Northern Virginia, 31, 66
artist, 44

bachelor, 21, 63-64
Baltimore, 32, 37, 54-56, 64
battle of:
    Chancellorsville, 22, 57
    Fredericksburg, 32-33, 57
    Gettysburg, 37, 41, 57, 66
    Malvern Hill, 45-46
    Second Manassas, 22, 41
beef, 36
best generals, 15
biscuits, 27
Bobby Lee (puppy), 45
brandy, 18
Brandy Station, 53
Brooklyn, 27, 58
Brown, John, 67
buttons, 38

Caesar (Julius), 17
Caskie, Norvell, 21, 50
cavalry, 33, 41, 53
Chesapeake and Ohio, 52
chickens, 25
children, 23

civilian, 38
Cocke, Charles, 62
Corbin Hall, 40
courtship/marriage, 21, 26, 35-36,
    41-42, 47-48, 53-54, 58-59, 63-
    64, 68-69
coward, 26-27
crows, 69
Culpeper, 21
Custis, Mary, 35
Custis Morgan (squirrel), 49

demijohn, 18, 25
Des Moines, 38
dignified, 18, 59
doctors, 37, 39, 61
ducks, 45

enemy, 22, 24, 36, 40, 46, 60, 68
England, 23
Esculapius, 39

faculty, 17, 52
fasting, 15
Fort Hamilton, 27, 30, 58
Fort Monroe, 64
Fredericksburg, 68
frogs, 50

Gaines, Gen. Edmund Pendleton,
    59
Gettysburg, 66
Gilderoy, 21
girls, 23, 54, 63-64
Gordon, Gen. John B., 65
Grant, Gen. Ulysses S., 31, 41, 46,
    65, 67

Hagerstown, 66